C000155655

MENTAL TOUGHNESS FOR BEGINNERS

Develop a Growth Mindset, Achieve an Unbeatable Mentality, Train Your Brain to Increase Self-Esteem and Self-Discipline in Your Life

Sarah Miller

TABLE OF CONTENTS

Introduction 1

Chapter 1 *Defining Mental Toughness* 3

Chapter 2 *Finding Your Identity* 9

Chapter 3 *Building Personal Resilience* 17

Chapter 4 *Strengthening Your Support System* 28

Chapter 5 *Bend, Don't Break* 38

Chapter 6 *Tough For Life* 46

Conclusion 62

Description 64

INTRODUCTION

Welcome, and thanks for purchasing *Mental Toughness for Beginners*, a primer for anyone who has ever wanted to learn about building resiliency, handling everyday stress, and bouncing back from all of life's unexpected obstacles. We all know that life is what you make of it, and if life is getting you down, how can you learn to roll with the punches, pick yourself up, and carry on?

In this book, we'll take a close look at defining mental toughness. You'll learn about the personality traits that make a person 'tough', and how to differentiate toughness from apathy because being resilient doesn't mean being unfeeling. We'll talk about finding your identity and ways to stand up for yourself without compromising your personal values. Learning to find that balance is crucial to being mentally tough. We'll also talk about how your mental health can affect your ability to be resilient, and what to do if you think you need outside help on your journey.

We'll also discuss how you can take small steps every day to alleviate stress and become more resilient to the stimuli you can't control. Are you someone that freaks out when the bus is running a little late in the morning, or do you calmly come up with a solution and find a way to get to work without ruining your whole day? That's the difference between someone without and someone with mental resilience! It doesn't mean you can't be upset about the bus, but it does mean you don't let it affect your entire existence.

Maybe you think that being mentally tough means you have to be an island; that in order to be tough, you need to be solitary and rely only upon yourself. This couldn't be further from the truth! People who are resilient can surround themselves with other like-minded people to build each other up and be a support system. While it's important to know that you *can* be self-reliant, it's equally important to know that you don't *have* to be. Having a support system to lean on can be the difference between resolving a difficult issue or being mired in self-doubt and paralyzed by anxiety or stress.

You're going to find a lot of information on being mindful, what that means, and how you can apply mindfulness to your life for the betterment of yourself and the benefit of others. We'll also talk about forgiveness and acceptance, how to make mistakes and make amends, and how to set important emotional boundaries. You'll also discover why personal accountability is so crucial to your journey towards resiliency.

Mental Toughness for Beginners is a complete how-to book that will walk you from discovering the core of your character and values to determine the best way to build your personal resiliency. As you go through the following chapters, you'll find exercises to help you define yourself and your beliefs, you'll learn how to cultivate the traits you want to strengthen and break the habits that keep you in the cycle of stress and self-doubt. You'll discover ways to handle everyday situations with grace and strength and learn how to deal with unexpected issues without losing yourself in the process.

When you're done with this book, you'll have a solid understanding of who you are, what you believe in, who your true friends are (or should be!), and what to do when life seems determined to drag you down. If you're excited to build your mental toughness, what are you waiting for? Let's head over to Chapter 1 and get started!

CHAPTER 1
Defining Mental Toughness

We're going to start your journey to greater mental toughness by defining what the term means, and what it means to you. Many times, the thought of mental toughness brings to mind someone who may be unfeeling or callous. Perhaps you may think that toughness means apathy. I assure you, it does not. People who are mentally tough don't lack feeling or emotion; they just have the ability to process their emotions, make a decision on what to do with those feelings, and plan a course of action that handles their situation with grace and strength. It is often, only after all is said and done that a mentally-tough individual takes the time to go back and let themselves be emotional. People who exhibit mental toughness know how to compartmentalize their emotions and their actions to take care of business, and then handle their emotions properly later.

Let's define toughness. The dictionary says that toughness is, "the state of being capable of handling rough treatment or adverse conditions." That's what people who are mentally tough show us- that no matter what life sends their way, they can handle it. Mentally tough people are those who know that it's okay to be emotional, but that you can't live in that adverse space. You have to take care of your stressors with your head, not your heart, and then use your heart to heal your head when the stressors come to an end or begin to improve. Another word for mental toughness is resilience- the ability to bounce back after a negative event. This ability to recover is one of the things we'll explore in-depth throughout the book.

Common Characteristics of Mentally-Tough Personalities

Think about the people you know whom you would consider to be mentally tough. When you examine their personalities, what are some traits that you see in common? Every person who is mentally resilient has commonalities with the others, and if you look closely (or sometimes not so closely), you see them. We're going to look at several of those traits, which will help you begin to form a picture of what you will need to do to attain resiliency.

Creating Strong Boundaries

People who are mentally tough or resilient (we'll use the terms interchangeably) are those that know their limits. They know when to walk away from unhealthy relationships or situations before they lose themselves. That doesn't mean that they don't go back and work on the problem at a later time, but that they know when to say enough is enough.

By establishing strong personal boundaries, people who are mentally tough keep themselves in control of every situation. They aren't used or abused by others who would take advantage of them.

By exhibiting the ability to know their limits, resilient people show others that they aren't to be trifled with. People will soon learn that they can't take advantage of the person with strong boundaries. If you can develop this skill, you may find that some people don't like you very much anymore- but here's the thing- they probably weren't your friend to begin with, sadly. When you work on your resiliency, you are going to find those false friends who will flee. That's okay! You don't want them anyway.

Having Strong Self-Awareness and Self-Esteem

Self-awareness and self-esteem go hand-in-hand in the realm of mental toughness. Knowing who you are and liking yourself are HUGE components of resiliency. For instance, you're already exhibiting self-awareness by reading this book! You are aware that you aren't as mentally tough as you'd like to be, and you are consuming this information to help yourself make a change.

Self-awareness is what tells about our personalities. Maybe you're not the smartest guy in the room. That's okay, as long as you know your capabilities and are willing to work to improve them. Being able to say, "I'm not great at math, but I know how to use these formulas, and I'm willing to work hard" is a great example of healthy self-awareness. The same goes for mental toughness. You might not have it yet, but you can, and you will!

Self-esteem is the second facet of self-awareness. You might know exactly who you are, but how do you feel about that? DO you like yourself? If so, why? If no, why not? Being able to objectively look at your traits is a great way to improve both your self-awareness and self-esteem. People who are resilient are confident in both of these aspects. They have a strong sense of self and a genuine liking for themselves. If they find there is something they don't like, they work to make a change. This internal toughness leads to a cycle of external resiliency.

Embracing a Sense of Impermanence

Resilient people have a strong sense of impermanence. No, we don't mean existential dread, although that's not to be discounted. By this turn of phrase, what we mean is that resilient people know that nothing is forever, even negative stressors. As many a wise grandmother has said, "this too shall pass." Mentally tough people know that no situation, no matter how good or bad, is permanent.

When you can set aside your immediate stress and begin to see the big picture, you can have a clearer sense of what you'll need to do to get from Point A of a stressful situation to Point B, where things begin to improve, to Point C, where the situation is resolved. It's almost a 'forest through the trees' scenario. Stepping back and thinking critically about how long a negative occurrence will affect you will give you clarity. Will it be a big deal tomorrow? A week, a month, a year, a decade from now? These are some of the questions that resilient people ask themselves to find perspective and solve their problems.

Maintaining Enriching Relationships

Another thing that mentally tough people have in common is that they don't do it alone. Resilient people have a support system, and we'll go into a lot of detail about that later, but it's an important component of a resilient life. It makes a lot of sense that those who are self-aware would also be highly aware of the people they have around them.

Have you ever been in a work scenario where you just didn't jive with a close co-worker? Maybe they didn't pull their weight or were negative or gossipy. It's difficult to be productive when you feel like you're being dragged down by someone who is supposed to be your teammate. When you have colleagues that you have mutual respect with and for, you can get your work done efficiently and effectively. You aren't wasting emotional energy on handling the co-worker; you're spending all your effort where it should be spent- on your work. The same thing goes for who you surround yourself with in all aspects of your life. When you're not spending time and emotional currency on the wrong people, you have much more energy and focus to deal with unexpected stress.

Practicing Mindfulness

If mindfulness feels like a buzzword these days, that's because it is. But the truth is that mindfulness practices have been around for centuries, and we're only now finding out how effective it is for the general population. Now that the secret is out, think about the resilient people you know. Are they out of touch with their lives, or are they in tune with what's going on in their own inner circle and beyond? Resilient people are mindful people- they use their powers of self-discipline and observation to make decisions and draw conclusions about the world around them.

When we're feeling low or uncertain, it's a natural human response to resort to extremes. We withdraw into ourselves, ignoring everything that's going on outside our heads because it's just too much to bear. Conversely, some people go wild- seeking escapism in partying and avoiding consequences. It's the people who are resilient that can maintain a grasp on reality and clear thinking, and those are the mindful ones.

Having Healthy Outlets

Drawing off that last trait, resilient people are those who have healthy outlets for their negative feelings. Instead of going to the extremes of hiding or losing all sense of inhibition and consequences, resilient people take care of their emotions through activities like hobbies, journaling, and even going to therapy- it's all about that self-awareness trait. The latest term for this type of behavior is self-care. Self-care, or whatever you'd like to call it, is a vital part of being able to recharge emotional batteries and heal the mind from stress and anxiety.

Healthy outlets are a hallmark of those who are mentally tough. Think about when you're under a lot of stress- what's your go-to activity? If you don't have a way to blow off steam or work out your emotions in a safe space, then you're putting up a mental obstacle to becoming more resilient. Removing those roadblocks will go a long way to building mental toughness and handling stress with fewer long-term effects.

Acknowledging Ignorance

Mentally-tough people know what they don't know, and they are strong enough to admit it. "I don't know" is one of the most difficult things that people can say because no one wants to look ignorant. But by being able to say, "I'm not sure," resilient people are showing their self-awareness. It's the next step of the conversation that may be more important, though, and that's the phrase, "but I can help you find out/I'll find out for you." This acknowledges that the person doesn't have all the answers at the moment, but that they are resourceful enough to remedy their own ignorance.

Resilient people aren't afraid to acknowledge that there may be a gap in their information because they trust themselves to learn the answer and to study harder next time. They are nonplussed by questions they can't immediately answer because they are confident in their ability to follow up. People who struggle with resiliency tend to get flustered when asked something they don't have an absolute for, and it can lead to a spiral of anxiety and negative thinking. Which leads us to our last common trait of people with mental toughness.

Moving on From Mistakes

People with mental resilience don't let their 'mistakes' define them. We're putting mistakes in quotes here because there are many levels of mistakes, and it's entirely subjective on a personal level. To be clear, we are not talking about the kinds of actions that negatively, permanently affect other people. Forgetting that your co-worker likes sugar in her coffee and murdering your co-worker are two very different things. A mentally tough person will apologize for the coffee mistake and move on. They'll remember for next time.

Someone without resiliency will worry about that coffee for a long time. They may even be concerned that they've permanently damaged their relationship with their colleague. This is a sign of anxiety and inappropriate stress management. If you want to improve your resiliency, you'll need to learn how to manage micro-stresses and not live in your minor mistakes. The more energy you spend on these kinds of worries, the less energy you will have to be positive and keep moving forward.

Mental Toughness in Action

It's easy to talk about the characteristics of resilient people, but sometimes it's difficult to put the whole picture together. The world is full of the stories of people who were faced with unexpected and unusual stressors, but found a way to emerge not unscathed, but able to recover and endure.

Take the story of Aron Ralston, the hiker, and rock-climber who amputated his own arm when he became trapped by a boulder in the Canyonlands National Park in the state of Utah. After more than three days stuck between the rock and the canyon wall, Ralston broke his own arm and used a pocket tool to remove the hand and forearm. His story was documented in a major motion picture in 2010, starring actor James Franco. Ralston survived the initial accident by using near-surreal critical thinking skills and courage.

But what's most resilient about this young man is that he continues to climb today and has become a motivational speaker and environmental advocate. Ralston did not let his accident stop him from doing what he loves, and while he *is* defined as the guy who cut off his own arm, it is not a negative label. Ralston's resiliency did not result from his accident but manifested from his already resilient nature. And that's a big key to putting mental toughness into action- having the skill set and the emotional resources BEFORE they are needed.

There are many other examples like this to be found, like professional surfer Bethany Hamilton, who lost an arm in a shark attack and continues to inspire young women worldwide to take up surfing. Warrick Dunn, a retired NFL player, who took the pain of the murder of his single mother when he was 18 and turned his career earnings into a foundation that facilitates homeownership for struggling single-parent families.

These are just a sample of the resilience that goes on in the world every day, but you don't have to look to celebrities or athletes to see examples of mental toughness. Did you have an adult in your life growing up that went above and beyond to take care of others and themselves despite not having the best circumstances? That's a show of resiliency. Look to people who are recovering from substance abuse issues and rebuilding their lives. These people are living a resilient lifestyle. You can see real-life examples of mental toughness in every aspect of your life. These are the people you should be examining when you're trying to define the common traits of resilient people.

One of the first things we talked about in this chapter is self-awareness and self-esteem, and in the next chapter, we're going to dive into the process of finding and defining identity. Without a strong sense of self, it's impossible to have a basis on which to build mental toughness, so let's go take a look at that endeavor and get you on your way to a more resilient mindset.

CHAPTER 2
Finding Your Identity

Who are you? Of course, you know your own name. You know where you live; you know your social security or government identification number. You recognize your face in the mirror and can recite your birthday. But do you know who you really are at the core? Do you know how to define yourself and your values and beliefs? Without a solid sense of self, you won't be able to work on building your resiliency, so let's dive into some ways that you can learn how to characterize yourself and what you believe in. You may want to grab a pencil and paper before you keep reading- we're going to be doing some brainstorming and making some lists throughout the rest of this chapter.

Identifying Beliefs and Values

One of the first steps in defining your identity is to identify your beliefs and your values. These are the basis of your personal principles, and they are crucial to your identity and your interactions with yourself and with others. You can have belief in many things, and the values that accompany those beliefs will be your guidebook to living the life you want to live.

When you think about a belief system, you may immediately leap to something like organized religion, political leanings, or even conspiracy theories. Those are all valid and very real sets of beliefs, and if you ascribe to any or all, get your paper and write them down as topic headings. Now, jot down some of the things from each topic that you firmly believe in- things in which you have utter, unshakeable faith. These items are the basis of your external beliefs. These are principles that you speak about and share with other people- other members of your religion or political party, those who you want to explain or argue those beliefs to, and to others who may wish to know more about you.

The second part of this exercise is to tie together those external beliefs with the values they represent. If you are a practicing Christian, then you have a belief in Jesus Christ as your savior. What values stem from that belief? For many Christians, these would be things such as charity, compassion, gratitude, and kindness. As you think about and write down your beliefs, you can then extend that into attributing values to those beliefs. What will emerge when you've finished your lists is a comprehensive overview of all your external beliefs and values.

After you've worked on putting your external beliefs and values in writing, it's time to think about your internal beliefs. It can be difficult to honestly assess our self-belief because sometimes, we can find out some painful truths about how we really feel. It's important that you are willing to examine your feelings and your self-talk. Self-talk is our inner monologue; it's that voice inside our heads that we use to talk to ourselves, sometimes even aloud when we think we're alone. The tone you use in your self-talk speaks volumes about your self-belief and self-esteem.

In the last chapter, we briefly talked about self-awareness and self-esteem being a commonality among resilient people. One component of this commonality is positive self-talk. Think about how you communicate with yourself. When you've made a mistake, do you berate yourself and refuse to let it go? Or do you comfort yourself and make a mental note to learn from your mistakes? The difference between scolding and reassurance is the difference between negative and positive self-talk.

Another good way to express the dichotomy between positive and negative self-talk is to imagine that you're getting dressed up for a night out. It's your friend's birthday, you're heading to an amazing restaurant, and then out to a nice lounge for drinks. Fun, right? So you rifle through the closet, pick out the perfect outfit, and stand in front of the mirror. What's your first thought? If it's critical (Ugh, I look fat!), then you're using negative self-talk. If it's complimentary (Wow, this shirt makes my eyes stand out!), then you're using positive self-talk.

So how does self-talk tie into self-awareness, self-esteem, beliefs, and values? Self-talk is the building block upon which all the rest are built. When you think honestly and objectively about how you talk to yourself, is it mostly positive or mostly negative? This leads to self-awareness; why do you talk to yourself the way you do? Once you've figured out why you're using that tone, you can determine whether or not you've got good self-esteem. And if you've got low self-esteem, then chances are good that you don't have much belief in yourself and your abilities. Without solid beliefs, how can you know what your values are?

That was a lot of questions, so take a few minutes to absorb and comprehend the link from self-talk to values, and once you've given it some thought, start writing. Write down the beliefs you have in yourself, and be specific- even if they are negative. It's okay to write, "I believe I'm not very good at _____." That's a belief to you. You feel that to be true, and it doesn't matter if you are the only one who feels that way; this is a list of your beliefs, no one else's. Be sure to list as many internal beliefs as you can think of, and then put your pencil down and walk away for a few minutes. Self-analysis is tough, emotionally tiring work. Go take a break.

When you come back, look at the list you made. Where are you using negative and positive self-talk? Can you frame any of your negative beliefs in a positive light? Doing so can help boost your self-esteem. Instead of saying, "I believe I'm not very good at _____," say, "I believe I can improve at _____." You're acknowledging an inadequacy (self-awareness) in positive self-talk, which will raise your self-esteem. Now, attach a value to your new belief. What value would you need to accompany a belief that you can improve at a certain skill? Perhaps you'd want the values of work ethic, perseverance, patience, or open-mindedness, depending on the area in which you want to improve.

If you can find a way to phrase even your most negative self-beliefs into positive language, congratulations! You've taken the first step in your journey towards resiliency. If you can speak to and of yourself with positivity, you are more likely to have higher self-esteem and less likely to take it personally when someone else says something negative to or about you. Now that you've defined both your internal and external beliefs and values, it's time to think about which of these principles you'd like to be the most dominant in your life.

Identifying Your Priorities

Have you ever been told or told yourself to "get your priorities straight"? That's a phrase that can get our hackles up, isn't it? No one likes to be told that they're focusing on the wrong thing, but hearing we need to get our priorities straight can be a much-needed wake-up call. Part of developing resilience is being able to determine what the most important things are in your life. This will help you know which things are worth fighting for, getting stressed out about, and working to remedy, and which things you should just let go.

In the last chapter, we talked about how a commonality of resilient people is to not live in their mistakes. This is because they know they can learn and grow from the experience instead of dwelling on the error. Much is the same with knowing your priorities. When you are confident in what's important to you, it's easy to move past things that are not. You can give them the time of day, process them, and then never think about them again because they do not affect your big picture. That doesn't mean that you're callous to happenings beyond your life bubble, but just because you are aware of something doesn't mean you have to react or respond.

Grab your paper and pencil again, and draw a dot in the middle of the page. Label it "me." That's you, in the center of your reality. Now draw a small circle around yourself, and in that circle, you're going to write the things that are the nearest and most dear to you. This inner circle should list the things in your life that you feel you cannot live without- your family, your faith, your hobbies, etc. This is the circle of people and activities that you would feel lost without or grieve the most if you were to lose. You can write individual names or places or things, and don't worry about hurting anyone's feelings. This is a private exercise for your eyes, heart, and brain only.

When you've finished making a list for your inner circle, draw another larger circle. This next circle is for the things and people you really love, but that might not be the end of the world if you lost. You might list your job here because you like it, but you can get another one or a club that you like attending but maybe isn't your number one hobby. You get the idea. You're going to keep drawing circles until you've gotten to the outside of your page. That last outer circle should be important things that you're cognizant of, but that you feel doesn't affect your everyday life. Remember, these are your priority circles, no one else's. You may love arguing politics, and it could be a core principle for you, so you'd put your political beliefs in your first or second circle. Someone else may abhor politics and put it in their outer circle- aware of its existence, but completely uninterested in engaging.

Another way to think about your priorities is to think about how you would react if certain things in your life were threatened. We hear the phrase, "I would kill for that!" used casually in response to material things, but when it comes to the people, beliefs, and values that we hold dearest in our inner circle, which would we (not literally, please) kill for? What are the things in your life that you will defend without a second thought?

You have to remember to include yourself on your list of priorities, too. It is not selfish to set boundaries and take care of yourself. You can make yourself a priority and still have plenty of emotional energy to take care of others. Having a strong, inviolable sense of self will actually make you a better co-worker, family member, neighbor, and friend. You will put your time and energy into the people and activities that are the most important and impactful to you and those around you, and you will find yourself able to say no to those who would take advantage of you or try to rope you into things you're uncomfortable with. Indeed, having your priorities set is a healthy, strong way to be more resilient.

One great thing about priorities is that they are flexible. You may be in a financial rut right now, and although you're not crazy about your job, you have to make it a priority because you need the money. In a couple of years, you could have a better job with higher pay, and you'll be able to shift your priorities around to include more leisure activities or going back to school, or other things you had to reluctantly relegate to the outer circles before.

When you take time to regularly assess and reassess your priorities, you'll begin to notice a shift in the way you think and feel about what's truly important in your life. You will be more confident in yourself, your beliefs and values, and have a stronger sense of self-worth, which are all qualities of mentally tough people.

Identifying Your Strengths and Weaknesses

This chapter is all about finding and defining yourself, and yes, that's going to mean you'll have to look at things a little critically. In previous segments, we talked about identifying beliefs and values and laying out your priorities. We also discussed positive self-talk and building self-esteem by adjusting your self-talk language. Here, we'll begin to tie those concepts together to be able to think objectively about your strengths and weaknesses, so we can finish up the chapter later by identifying and setting goals.

Before you begin making lists and potentially feeling bad about yourself because you are thinking about weaknesses, remember two things. This exercise is about self-awareness (a resiliency commonality) and turning negatives into positives (a self-talk and self-esteem booster). It's really important to be able to be honest with yourself, or you'll never be able to achieve the sort of self-improvement that you're seeking on your road to mental toughness. You can't make a road map to where you're going without knowing where you're starting, and this is what his exercise is about.

When you're ready for some inner reflection, it's time to make the list that's going to eventually evolve into your resiliency goals. For now, you're just going to write down what you perceive to be your weaknesses. It doesn't matter if they are rational, irrational, significant, or seemingly trivial. Just write it all down. Get it out of your system and onto a piece of paper. You'll find it's actually very therapeutic.

Next, take a deep breath and write down what you perceive to be your strengths. Again, this can be anything you think that you do well. This is more of a stream of consciousness exercise than anything else. You want to think critically about what you are good at, in your work life, home life, and in the community. Think about the qualities that make you inherently you. What do you like, no- love- about yourself? This is all about the power of positivity, so list anything and everything you can think of.

Once you've written yourself dry, look at the lists. If you've got a giant mess of scribbling and messy blurbs everywhere, take the time to rewrite what you've accumulated. Make one column of perceived strengths and one column of perceived weaknesses. Can you make any correlations between the two lists? If so, how? Yes, this is a critical thinking exercise. You want to make connections from the things you are good at to the things you feel you need to improve. Look to see if there are any corresponding qualities between the two lists. These can be things that are complete opposites or things that are in the same vein. The connections can be between skills or personality traits. You are just looking to round out your personal assessment.

When you've taken a good look at the lists and made your correlations, now it's time to think about how you can use those connections to your advantage. Do you feel like you've got strengths and weaknesses that fall into the 'same skill set' category? If so, why do you think you're good at one thing in that skillset, but not the other. This could be for reasons like less experience, practice, or familiarity, which you can choose to work on, or lack of interest or desire to improve. That's okay, but ask yourself- if it

13

wasn't a priority for me to work on, why was it important enough for me to think of when I was writing my list of weaknesses?

Just so you know, it's okay to take a break when you're working on this type of deep self-reflection. You can write your lists and go take a walk to revisit them with a clear head. You can sleep on them and try again in the morning. Remember, part of being resilient is being able to set boundaries, so people don't use you as a doormat. Don't make yourself a doormat, either. These exercises are important, but the reason you're doing them is to build mental toughness. It's okay to not be mentally tough enough to get through them in one sitting the first time! Just don't put them off so long; you lose your sense of purpose.

The last step in examining your strengths and weaknesses is to find the positive in every list. We discussed this a little earlier when we went over positive and negative self-talk. Look at your list of weaknesses. Try to rephrase each one to have a positive spin. Instead of saying, "I lose my patience too quickly," try, "I'm working on being more patient." Swap out, "I'm not a great listener," with, "I'm aware that I need to listen better when my friends are talking." For each weakness that you can turn into a more positive statement, you are already one step closer to building those skills, finding better self-awareness, and creating goals for yourself.

Of course, you're reading this book because you want to learn about building mental toughness. Maybe you're wondering how fiddling around with strengths and weaknesses can lead to better resiliency. There are a few factors at play here. The first is to learn better self-awareness, one of those common traits of mentally tough people. The second is to learn better self-talk, which leads to better self-esteem. If you don't respect yourself, no one else will respect you either. The third is because we are our own worst critics. Chances are very good that many of the flaws you see in yourself aren't seen through the eyes of others. If you can handle a bunch of self-reflection and survive, you can handle anything that anyone else throws at you.

There's a lot more to building resiliency than that, but knowing what you think your strengths and weaknesses are and what you can do to reconsider the way you phrase things and talk to yourself goes a long way towards establishing our next step, and that's going to be setting some resiliency goals for yourself. You're going to take what you've learned in the last few segments and put it all together to figure out what it is that you want to achieve, what habits you think you'd like to break, and what new habits you'd like to replace them with. Once you've set your goals, we'll then move into real-world activities, mental exercises, and mindfulness practices you can employ to reach those goals of resiliency.

Identifying and Setting Your Resilience Goals

What is it exactly that you want to achieve? Based on what you've come up with during the previous self-reflection exercises, you're going to make a list of SPECIFIC behaviors you want to exhibit. For many people, learning to be more resilient means to learn how to be more accepting of things you cannot change and knowing how to fight for the things you can. For others, being mentally tough means building thicker skin and learning how not to take things so personally. For others still, finding resiliency means discovering the strength within themselves to recover from long-term stress and trauma.

This is a personal journey. Only you can determine what your goals are, but no matter what you want to build or improve upon, there are some guidelines you can follow to set realistic, achievable goals for to build your resilient future:

1) Be specific in what you want to achieve. If one of your goals is to 'be less sensitive to stress,' then make sure you can identify exactly when, where, and how you experience the kind of stress that feels crippling. Is it stress at work? What situations make you feel overwhelmed and anxious? Now you can be more exacting in your goal.

Instead of being vague, say, "I want to learn how to not get overwhelmed when we have a deadline at work. I know the pressure from the boss isn't personal, so I need to be better about not taking it to heart."

That is a specific goal with defined parameters.

2) Be realistic. You want to set goals that are attainable, and you can do that by setting a series of short-term goals that lead into or add up to a single long-term goal. This also allows you to revamp your goals as you meet the milestones you've set for yourself. Learning resilience is a process and journey. You need to retrain your brain to be tough, and that doesn't happen instantly. Which leads to our next guideline:

3) Give yourself a timeframe. While learning to be resilient isn't a goal that can be measurable in terms of true tangibility, you want to be able to have benchmarks to compare your new behavioral responses to your responses in the past. You can make a point to reassess yourself once a month, every few months, and then check yourself after a year. If you are making progress, you will see and feel it in your self-assessment. Habits are difficult to break, but we're going to discuss what it takes to create healthier, more resilient behaviors in the next chapter.

4) Write your goals down and make sure you revisit them regularly. In the next chapter, we're going to talk a little bit about using mantras as reminders, and this will tie directly into putting your goals in writing. There's something about putting things in print that makes them seem more real. Use your written goals, your timeframe, and your milestones to create a specific plan of action.

5) Be kind to yourself. Mind your self-talk when you think you're not living up to your goals. Everyone has a bad day or a time when no matter how strong they want to be, they are just out of emotional energy. This is normal human behavior. No one is a resilient rock one-hundred percent of their lives, and if they say they are, they are either devoid of emotion or lying!

6) Be willing to adjust your goals. Sometimes life doesn't go as planned. Learning to be mentally tough is not the same as a more tangible goal, like saving to buy a car or getting a degree or certification. This is a personal journey, and sometimes personal journeys require rerouting. Reassess your goals regularly, and you'll be in good shape!

7) Pat yourself on the back when you achieve a milestone! We often don't give ourselves enough credit for the things we've accomplished that aren't something concrete or measurable. It's a huge thing to be able to look back and see how far you've come! Just because there is no printed certificate for resiliency doesn't mean you don't deserve to celebrate.

When you've set your *specific* behavioral goals, it's time to get to work on them! In the next chapter, we'll be looking at mindfulness and mantras, quick mental exercises for relieving immediate stress, and long-term behavioral exercises for breaking bad habits and creating new ones- all designed to help you reach your resiliency goals.

CHAPTER 3
Building Personal Resilience

By this point, you've been asked to do a lot of self-analysis, which is a lot of hard emotional work. Now it's time to take everything you've learned about yourself and poured into your goals and set your plan into motion. In this chapter, we're going to be looking at specific ways that you can build your resiliency for real, noticeable results. It all starts with being able to retrain your brain and ends with being able to draw emotional boundaries and overcome stressful situations, both short- and long-term, without feeling like you are compromising your values or your self-esteem.

Making and Breaking Mental Habits- The World Inside Your Head

Habits are the behaviors that make up our everyday life. While we tend to think of habits with a negative connotation, that's not always the case. We have tons of good habits- things like brushing our teeth every morning or changing our sheets once a week, or even saying "please" and "thank you" when we want and receive something. Habits can be defined as behaviors we repeat without needing to be prompted because they are ingrained in our thought pattern or daily routine.

There are of course bad habits as well. We see nail-biting and hair-twirling in children. Adults can fall into patterns of unhealthy eating or take up habits like smoking or drinking that can evolve into chemical addictions. Let's talk about that for a minute, because the brain patterns that result from substance use are actually a change in the neural pathways. The brain becomes used to these substances attaching to the neural transmitters, and the chemistry of the brain is altered.

The same is true of habits. Habits are based on a reward system. When you brush your teeth, you don't get cavities. When you say "please," you have a much better chance of getting what you want than if you were rude. When you get your reward, you feel good, and when you feel good, your brain releases its happy chemicals- dopamine, oxytocin, serotonin, and endorphins- and you can get addicted to them! It's fascinating neuroscience; the same things happen to your brain chemistry when you become addicted to good things as when you get addicted to bad things. So what does this have to do with mental toughness?

The answer is that you want your brain to be on the good side of this "addiction equation." When you lack resilience, you can get caught in a vicious cycle of unhappiness. You don't know how to draw yourself out a stress-induced funk. You'll find yourself apologizing for things that aren't your fault and compromising your values so that you don't rock the boat.

In other words, you'll lose your self-esteem and your boundaries, and as we know, you need good self-esteem and healthy boundaries for mental toughness.

Before we go into specific techniques for building resiliency, let's pause for a minute to consider this: If you are struggling with anxiety or depression and you think that you need professional assistance, please don't hesitate to reach out to resources in your community. Even if you are uninsured or underinsured, you will be able to find free or low-cost options to help you get healthy. Call your local government's social services department, or reach out to the support group coordinator at your local hospital. These are places you will be able to find the resources you need to manage your mental health.

With that said, in the next few segments, we're going to talk about methods you can use to discover even more about yourself, break down and rebuild neural pathways to accommodate new habits and ways of thinking, and deal with your stress and the stress that others put on your plate. If you keep thinking about habits specifically as a set of learned behaviors, it will be easier to think about changing those behaviors and altering your brain chemistry for good.

Making Time for Mindfulness

When we talked about the common traits of resilient people, we touched upon their exhibition of mindfulness. This is a vital component of being both self-aware and situationally aware and will help you build a better relationship with yourself and your world. Being mindful means to live in the present, to be able to think about nothing else but the moment at hand, and being cognizant of your feelings and the feelings of those around you.

One of the biggest factors that can lead to undue stress and lingering bad feelings can be miscommunication. Humans are strange creatures- we often tell untruths to avoid hurting feelings or causing embarrassment to ourselves or others, but our mouths and our body language say two very different things. When your brain finally makes the connection, you can have an 'aha!' moment, and you begin to berate yourself for not reading the situation correctly as it occurred. Not being able to pick up non-verbal cues can cause a lot of discomfort, and in extreme circumstances, it can divert the course of an entire relationship.

Many people think of mindfulness as a meditation technique, and it can be. You can learn about long-form mindfulness exercises if that's something that interests you, but for our purposes, we're going to talk mostly about being observant on the daily and discovering how to read the people around you and trust yourself and your judgment about how you fit into the big picture of your life. When you can be aware and self-aware enough to handle scenarios as they unfold, you will be able to apply that same awareness to yourself when you need to be mentally tough.

Here's something you can try on your way to work or school in the morning: counting cars. The theory is that you are so ingrained into your commuting routine, you've ceased to think about anything else. If you take a bus or train to work, give yourself something to look for, like a little personal game of Eye Spy. Count how many broken tiles you see on the subway tunnel wall at each station. Count how many stop signs your bus goes past. If you drive, count how many blue cars you see on your way. You can count squirrels if you walk. You get the idea. The concept is to draw you out of your habitual rut and OBSERVE the things around you. When you choose something to look for, you'll be amazed at what you see.

Another thing to do is quiz yourself with trivia about the people around you. You walk past the reception desk every morning. What color are the security guard's eyes? You probably greet this person like an old friend each day, but how observant have you been? This is all a part of observational mindfulness. The better you get at it, the better you will be at predicting the behavior of the people you see every day. You'll learn how to read their facial expressions and body language. When you can predict how other people will act, you can adjust your behavior accordingly. Like a poker player reading the tells of his opponent, you can read the non-verbal communication from your family, friends, and colleagues. And like that poker player, you'll also be at an advantage.

What about mindfulness for learning more about yourself and being able to alter your habits? That's the second part of the mindfulness equation. It's great to be situationally aware, but you need self-awareness, too. To get the point across in this respect, we're going to suggest you snitch on yourself. Yes, be a tattletale about yourself to yourself. Be deliberate in your actions. When you catch yourself exhibiting a bad habit, tell on yourself! Make a point of calling yourself out for your undesired behavior. For instance, if you've set a goal of not letting work stress cause you undue anxiety, snitch on yourself when you feel anxiety welling up. That's not to say you need to berate yourself into oblivion about every little thing, but make yourself aware of your behavior. Tell yourself, "Hey, I feel that stressful feeling coming on, but there's nothing to be stressed about right now. I got this!"

The more mindful you are about calling yourself out, the quicker you will be able to permanently change the behavior. Psychologists say that, on average, it takes ten weeks to break or form a permanent habit, although you should be discouraged if it takes longer. The more you work at being mindful and recognizing your behavior for what it is, the more fluent your new habit will become, and your old habit will be left in the dust.

Here is a quick mindfulness and centering exercise you can use if your pep talks to yourself aren't enough. When you're feeling stress or anxiety about to hit, and you can't seem to quell it, try the 5-4-3-2-1 grounding exercise. Take a few deep breaths and look around. Find five things you can see and describe them to yourself. Next, try to identify four things you could feel, like the fabric of your chair or the soft cotton of the draperies.

After that, look for three things you can hear, like a bird singing or traffic going by. Then you'll identify two things you can smell, like coffee brewing or a coworker's cologne. The last thing you'll do is name one thing you like about yourself, to finish the exercise on a positive note. Once you've run through this grounding technique, you'll find that your brain is reset, and you can begin to relax and get back to business. By forcing yourself to only think about the world around you at that very moment, it allows your stress levels to go down and your body to begin self-regulating properly again.

Keep working on your habits, and you'll begin to see a marked change in your behavior. Call yourself out when you're not acting the way you want to act, and keep yourself grounded with everyday mindfulness techniques. You will find that when you live a mindful life, you'll become more in tune with your own feelings and be more intuitive about the feelings of other people. That situational awareness will take you a long way towards reaching your resiliency goals.

Making Use of Mantras

In the last segment, we talked about snitching on yourself when you catch an undesired behavior. You can also be proactive with a little self-propaganda in the form of mantras. Mantras are short words and phrases that can remind us to do something, act a certain way, or behave according to a specific belief or value. Mantras are created from a larger belief statement or mission statement, drawing on key points to create brief, important reminders of our self-expectations and our goals.

To come up with effective mantras, it's crucial to first have a defined personal mission statement. It's time to get out that pen and paper again because we're going to re-examine the notes you made when you set your mental toughness goals. Writing a mission statement doesn't have to be a huge chore, and you've already done the work, you just don't know it!

A good mission statement is clear, concise, and states the values and goals that you want to uphold and achieve. You've surely seen the mission statements of various companies and organizations over the years. Let's take a crack at writing yours now. Look at the lists you made before and pick out your prioritized goals, beliefs, and values. The next step will be to put them all together into a paragraph. It could go something like this:

I know that I often let stress and worry overwhelm me at work. I want to be more resilient in the face of everyday pressure, and I am making an effort to be more mindful about my behavior and how I let the behavior of others affect me. Each day, I am spending time to remind myself that I am good at my job, that I won't compromise my integrity to appease the people who cause my stress, and that I will come out of this mental exercise stronger and more capable of standing up for myself. I am not a doormat, and I will set strong boundaries with those who want to treat me as such.

This mission statement clearly lays out the following criteria:

The problem: stress at work and demanding colleagues

The personal value: maintaining professional integrity

The pep-talk: "I am good at my job."

The goal: to set strong boundaries at work

The effort: being mindful and using positive self-talk

Looking at this mission statement, what would be some good mantras to draw from it? There are a few phrases that stand out, such as "I am good at my job" and "I am not a doormat." These few short words are strong and clearly convey the feelings behind the mission statement. When you use mantras to remind yourself to change how you think, you are making a commitment to not let yourself be affected by the thoughts and actions of others. You KNOW you are good at your job, and you know that the way others act is not a reflection on you, but on themselves. Use that knowledge to continue to build self-esteem and more positive self-talk. When you reach one set of goals, rewrite your mission statement and your mantras, and come up with new ones!

Mantras are great because you can say themselves to yourself anytime, anywhere. Take a deep breath, recite your mantra, and make your response to the stimuli that provoked it. You will find that these little blurbs will get you through your day, and you'll notice a marked improvement in your mood and your behavior. You may notice that others begin to act differently towards you as well, as you change. People who were previously used to walking all over you may not be thrilled to see you stand up for yourself. Too bad! That's on them, not on you. But conversely, you may find that your newfound confidence draws in other confident people with whom you can form lasting, positive relationships.

Making Molehills out of Mountains

Back when we talked about the common traits of resilient people, we talked about how they don't linger over their mistakes or stumbling blocks. That doesn't mean that they don't care; it means that they are able to see the big picture and where that obstacle fits in. When you're working on your resiliency skills, one of the things you'll need to learn is how to flip your behavior and turn molehills into mountains.

When something happens that you think you won't be able to handle, it can feel overwhelming and make you want to give up without trying. In order to become more resilient, you need to find a way. There's no promise that it will be easy, but here are some tips for taking what seems like an impossible problem and coming to an acceptable conclusion:

- Break things down into smaller pieces. Let's say that the problem is a banana. You're afraid to peel it because all the individual factors will come tumbling out. That may be true, but you also aren't going to eat an entire banana in one bite- you need to take it a bite at a time and chew it slowly. Such is the way to handle a large, problematic, or stressful undertaking. By breaking it down into small pieces, you can overcome one obstacle at a time to achieve the desired result.

- Analyze the impacts. When faced with something you think you might not be able to overcome or recover from, take the time to think about what will happen if you don't address the problem. What will be the short-, medium-, and long-term impacts of your action or inaction? It can help to write lists of pros and cons to each potential solution and think about what can happen tomorrow, next week, in a month, a year, or a decade from now. Will there be a significant long-term impact from your decisions? Once you've done your analysis, you can make a better choice about what needs or doesn't need to be done.

- Turn your brain into a filing cabinet. People who are resilient aren't unfeeling, they just know how to compartmentalize their emotions. Think about people who work under high stress in the medical field. A trauma surgeon must be both passionate and compassionate, but they must set aside all emotion when they are racing to save a patient. Once the surgery is complete, that surgeon can then reflect on what has happened and work through their emotions. Even if they go home and cry with pent-up frustration and sadness, they still get up and come back to work the next day to do it all over again. That's compartmentalizing in a nutshell and a grand example of why it is such a hallmark of the mentally tough.

- Minimize, don't trivialize. When you're thinking about how to react to a stressor, it's okay to be upset or emotional. You aren't required to pretend that nothing is wrong, but you want to find a way to minimize the impact that the stressor will have on your life. You can't continuously live in a state of stress; it's not healthy and will cause mental and physical health concerns. Instead, ask yourself to use your critical thinking skills to brainstorm ways to minimize the impacts of what's going on. If you can't get away unscathed, what's the acceptable collateral damage? You'll find that thinking about things from a strategic standpoint rather than a purely emotional one will save you from some of the long-term effects of major stress.

Handling Overwhelming Stimuli- The World Outside Your Head

There's a certain sense of satisfaction that comes from being able to look at a problem head-on and not crumble under the stress. In the first part of this chapter, we talked a lot about handling negative stimuli from within yourself, and we'll go into the last half of the chapter talking more in-depth about the stress that comes from outside sources and what you can do to handle it efficiently and without undue damage to yourself. It's also important to know when to write things off as 'not your problem' and know when to cut your losses and accept that some things will never change.

Handling Immediate Stress

Immediate stress is the kind that comes out of nowhere and hits you in the face. This can be an unexpected turn of events at work, an injury, or a personal loss. This kind of stress, which came through no fault of your own, can be upsetting and throw you for a loop. This can be tough even for the most resilient of people, so if you're still working on building your mental toughness, how can you handle immediate stress without wrecking your progress? Let's talk about the impacts of unexpected negative stimuli.

Being faced with immediate stress is a good way to determine how far you've come with your goals, although we certainly wouldn't wish undue stress on anyone. With that said, building resiliency is like building any other structure- you won't know how effective or strong it is until it's put through its paces. When stress comes flying at you, it can feel like a literal assault to the senses. You may lose your breath or feel shaky- that's your fight or flight response kicking in. To be resilient, you have to know when to fight and when to cut your losses.

If you already deal with anxiety or other mental stress concerns, you may already have an overactive fight or flight response. Learning to do some deep breathing can help you calm the immediate reaction to outside stress. Box breathing is a method taught to military and law enforcement to slow the body's stress response, and it's quite easy to learn. You simply empty your lungs and count to four. Then breathe in through your nose counting to four, hold your breath for a four-count, and then exhale for a count of four. Repeat the process four times, of course. This slows your racing heart rate and resets the oxygenation in your blood that results from shallow breathing when hit with unexpected stress.

Once you've calmed yourself enough to assess the situation, you can refer back to what you learned in the first half of this chapter. Practice your mantras and your pep-talks. Use what you've discovered about the power of compartmentalization, and especially try to analyze the impact. That's a huge key to being resilient in the face of crisis. You know that resilient people are aware that nothing is forever. Even the loss of a loved one, which is quite permanent, doesn't mean that you will feel the acute grief every day for the rest of your life. Dealing with unexpected stress can be hard-hitting, but you want to be tough enough for it to leave a bruise and not a scar.

If you analyze the situation and you find that there is no acceptable solution, you can choose to walk away before you can be permanently damaged. Say your significant other springs on you that they've been cheating, but they really want to work it out and stay together. You are going to feel bad. You are going to be hurt, and you are going to be angry, and yes, that is a situation that could leave a permanent mark on your psyche. You are allowed to say no. If you have analyzed the situation and you know that it will cause more harm than good for you to stay and work it out, then you are well within your rights to throw that partner out like yesterday's trash.

That's the thing about resiliency. You'll know when you've reached your goal, and unfortunately, it will come in the middle of a crisis. But finding the strength to be able to look at a scenario, examine the options, and do what is right FOR YOU is going to feel so good. You'll be able to work through the initial hurt and pain and be happy with the long-term decision you've made. And if you decide to work things out, the ball is in your court. You still have the personal power in the relationship to stand up for yourself and say, "This isn't okay."

The ability to say, "This isn't okay," is a great benchmark for your progress in building your mental toughness. If you were a person that would always agree or go along with things just to avoid conflict and then end up getting walked all over, being able to stand up for yourself is a huge step. If it's a work situation that's got you trying to improve your resiliency, then it may take your co-workers some adjustment to the new you- the one who doesn't clean up their every mess for them. It may be rough at first, but it will weed out the colleagues that respect you for you and those who only respect what you can do for them. Without your constant backup, they may finally get called out for their shortcomings, but that's not your problem. We promise.

When you become more effective at handling short-term stress and immediate stress, you will be a stronger person. Like anything else, the more your practice, the better you get. So don't be afraid to take a deep breath before you make any decisions. Don't be afraid to stand up for yourself. Don't be afraid to say, "This isn't okay." Do these things and exercise all the stress management techniques we've gone over, and you'll do just fine.

Handling Long-term Stress

Sometimes stress doesn't come quickly. Sometimes it does come quickly, but brings its luggage and unpacks for a long stay. It's important to learn some coping strategies for dealing with long-term stress events. This could be something like an illness in the family, an injury that requires a lengthy rehabilitation, or a major event at work that's going to take a while to work through. You've learned how to handle the sudden influx of immediate stress, but these long-term techniques will keep you moving through life as you navigate uncertain waters.

For starters, you need to make time to not be okay. If you are the primary caregiver for an unwell family member, it's okay to be strong all day and cry a little at night. Way back when we talked about the commonalities of resilient people, we said that they take time for self-care and have healthy outlets for their stress. That can mean having a hot shower and a good cry. When you spend all day under constant stress knowing that tomorrow will be the same thing again, it is easy to let pent-up sadness and anger eat at you. Let it out! Dams have spillways for a reason. They are there to let off excess pressure to stop the dam from breaking. Let your tears be a spillway.

Even if you spend your entire day shuttling between doctors' appointments and cooking meals and counting out medications, you still need a hobby. Set some time aside for yourself every night before bed to read or watch a favorite program. Join an online community for people in similar situations and talk to each other about hobbies and respite care. You'll be amazed at the resources you will find from others who are in the same boat as you. There will always be someone who has been paddling longer, and they will have a lot to teach you.

If you're the reason you are under stress, what to do? Let's say you had an accident, and now you're faced with long-term recovery. How can you keep your mental strength and not be too down on yourself and your situation? It's time to be your own best advocate. Try to stay on top of your recovery strategy; don't let anyone else make major decisions for you. Talk to your doctors and other health professionals, and don't be afraid to research new therapies on your own to discuss with them.

To keep yourself from boredom, anxiety, and other mental health detractors, stay busy even if you can't be mobile. If you have a hobby, find a way to do it while you recover. This can mean that even if you had an active hobby, you could get into a peripheral or related hobby while you convalesce. If you were an active boater, try building models. If you're an athlete, take the time that you can't play your sport to study it by reading biographies of your favorite players or delving deep into rules manuals. You could study game tapes and analyze them for your teammates. The point is, no matter what you did before, you should find a way to continue doing it for your own long-term mental health.

If the long-term stress you are experiencing is at work or school, try your best to leave it there. Yes, that's always easier said than done, but try to set boundaries. Tell yourself that you aren't going to answer emails after a certain time at night. Make your colleagues aware that you'll be turning your phone off when your kids go to bed. Don't make yourself unavailable for emergencies, but set clear parameters for what constitutes an emergency. Then make yourself follow the rules! If you're turning your phone off at ten, don't turn it back on at eleven just to take a peek. Watch TV, read a book, catch up on work paperwork if you must, but don't answer the phone and add to the workload.

If you're sensing a common theme between these scenarios, it's that taking care of yourself is vital to long-term mental health and resiliency.

You cannot pour from an empty cup, so you have to be able to rejuvenate yourself. You can still use all of your short-term coping strategies, too, because the more mental toughness you can build, the better. And if you find that dealing with long-term stress is just feeling like too much, find a counselor. You could look for a therapist or talk to the clergy at your place of worship. When you have an objective ear to listen to what's bothering you, you'll be surprised at how much better you will feel. That's the power of not feeling alone- it does wonders for resiliency.

You can also consider some new hobbies that are proven stress-relievers. Try a yoga class, and see if you like it. Map a route around your neighborhood that would be good for an evening walk or jog. Kickboxing is becoming popular in many areas and is a terrific stress relief workout. When you are dealing with the constant pressure of long-term stress, the best thing you can do to build and maintain resilience is to take care of yourself and find those healthy outlets for your negative feelings. So have an impromptu dance party with your kids, chat with your best friend, and set aside the stress for a while to renew your emotional energy and rest your brain and your soul for the next round.

Handling Everyone Else's Stress

We all want to be good friends, good coworkers, and good relatives and parents, so how do you help the people you care about when they are going through stressful situations without taking on so much of the burden that you, yourself, begin to feel undue stress? It's tough to be a caretaker when you're not sure if you can stay strong enough for the job. On a broader scale, how do you handle the stress and anxiety of the world as a whole? We are bombarded with bad news on the daily, and that sort of global turmoil can also take a toll on the psyche. The answer to both questions is to set healthy boundaries.

If you are trying to help someone close to you go through a painful time, it is crucial to protect your own emotions. When people are hurting, they sometimes aren't able to be aware of how much they are asking of other people. Sometimes you can feel capable of taking on all their pain, only to find out that you were wrong. In these scenarios, no one is really at fault, but this can all be avoided by setting boundaries. If you've got a friend going through a painful breakup, and all they want to do is talk to you about it, that's great! Everyone wants to feel needed. But it's okay to not answer their text message during dinner with your family, and you can tell them that. It's fine to say, "I love you, I am here for you, and I'll be back after I get the kids to bed." That is a healthy boundary that lets your friend know that you care, but you need time to handle your own business.

If you have a colleague that is going through a tough time, you need to set the same boundaries. Let's say they lose a parent, and there's a big deadline coming up. You're likely going to have to do some more work than you'd originally planned on, but it's okay. You want to be a good coworker, and you also need to meet the needs of the job. But there may come a time where that colleague comes back to work and needs to resume their duties. It's okay to tell them, "I'm so sorry for your loss, and I know you'll be ready to work again soon. I'll keep picking up the slack for now, but let's transition you back to your full duties by x date, so we don't lose productivity."

When you use kind, clear language, you are saying to your friend or colleague that you are drawing a line that is the point between you feeling helpful and you feeling taken advantage of. The setting of boundaries shows respect for yourself and others. You want to maintain a good relationship with the people in your inner circles, but without compromising the values and goals you've identified for yourself.

The stress bombarding us all on a global scale is another story, but you can use similar coping mechanisms to build and protect your mental toughness. You do not have to submit yourself to the 24-hour news cycle if you don't want to. You can establish rules for yourself regarding reading, watching, and listening to the news. Find a source that you trust and limit yourself to once-a-day consumption. In this ever changing world, it is important to stay informed, but it's not necessary to overwhelm yourself with so much bad news that it takes over your whole psyche.

The truth is that global turmoil has always been there; we just didn't have global news networks with satellite feeds. The technology that gives us the news at our fingertips is a double-edged sword. Turn it off if it feels like you're being stabbed. You have the freedom to consume as much or as little bad news as you can handle. And don't let yourself get to a breaking point before you make a change. Set those boundaries early and stick to them.

What happens when the outside stress is delivered straight to your door in the form of a natural disaster or town-wide scandal? Go back to square one with your immediate stress coping mechanisms and work through all your mental exercises. If it becomes a long-term situation, let your long-term strategies take over. Use your mantras, take care of yourself, and seek help if you find yourself overwhelmed and in need of counsel. The power of not feeling alone is never to be discounted, and that leads us to our next chapter. We'll be taking a deep dive into building a positive support system to help you build and maintain your resiliency so that you can deal with everything life throws your way.

CHAPTER 4
Strengthening Your Support System

The truth is, no matter how strong we feel, we can't do everything ourselves and maintain good mental and emotional health. We all want to believe that we are powerful enough to get through anything alone, and that's a great belief! It's important to have confidence in your ability to handle both short-term and long-term stress, and we talked about how to use positive self-talk to build up your self-esteem. Life isn't predictable, and there may be times when a sudden stressor arises, and you'll be the one who has to take care of it alone. But after that event is over and dealt with, you are going to need or want to tell someone else about it. Who are you going to tell?

Let's say you are in a long-term stress situation like we discussed in the last chapter. You may feel like you are alone, but if you think about it, you're not. If you are the primary caregiver for an ill loved one, you still have a medical team supporting you. If you're a single parent who is working more than one job and trying to make your way in the world as you raise your children, the school system is there to educate your children while you are at your job. The point is, a support system is crucial for everyone, no matter their circumstances. You want to find yours, identify the people who have a positive impact on your life, and find a way to rid yourself of people who would drag you down. This is going to require that you have the self-esteem necessary to say, 'forget you!' to the people who aren't contributing to your life in an uplifting way.

Identifying Your Support System

Think about the things you do every day. You are part of a system of humanity, and it's evident in every task that we complete and every place we visit. You may take a bus to work or drive on a highway. You didn't build the vehicle that provides you with transportation. You are likely not the mechanic that maintains it or part of the network of people who drill for, refine, and supply the gasoline or diesel that makes the vehicle run. You go to your place of work, and the lights are on because there are power plants staffed by people who produce the electricity and linesmen and electricians who make sure the power is delivered to you safely and efficiently.

Let's say you work in a restaurant or a grocery store. Did you and your coworkers produce all the food for sale? No, of course not. There is a system of farmers, wholesalers, and transporters responsible for the food on the shelves or on the tables. Everything we do is because someone else does their job, and other people are dependent on you to do yours. This is being part of the system of humanity. Very rare are the people who can live their lives without ever relying on another person for something else.

This is an important way to think about yourself as part of a greater human community, but it's also a good way to think about your mental and emotional health. You can be as strong as they come, but there will still come a time in your life that you will need another person to support you. There are a lot of different types of support, and you will find that you'll turn to a certain person or people for one kind, and to another person or group for another. Let's take a look at these different kinds of support and how they'll fit into your life.

Professional Support

Being able to rely on one's coworkers, colleagues, associates, and even competitors is something that can make your work life much more productive and successful. We're not saying that everyone you work with needs to be your best friend, but knowing that your boss has your back or that your desk-mate is supportive and has like-minded goals can go a long way. A lot of adults who report unhappiness with their jobs indicate that the work itself isn't the problem, but their coworkers or the business environment.

We hear a great deal about toxic workplaces today, and it's a fairly new turn of phrase to describe an old concept. A toxic work environment is one that makes you feel uncomfortable, often to the point of being unable to perform your job properly. This may be an atmosphere created by management or by your colleagues, but it's not good for your mental health. Studies show that people who work in healthy environments are more productive, more likely to stay in that workplace, and more apt to recommend employment there to other people.

Medical Support

Whether you are healthy as a horse or deal with chronic medical issues, having a medical support system in your life is really important. This means having doctors, nurses, technicians, and therapists that you trust to get you back to health or help you positively manage your conditions. Think about it. What would you do if you busted up your knee tomorrow? Do you know which hospital has the best emergency department? Can you get an appointment or a referral to an orthopedist right away? Who would you ask to help you find the best surgeon to put you back together? Not only are all those questions vital to knowing whether or not you've got a good medical support system, but you also need to consider who will take care of you after your surgery, where you will go for physical therapy, how you will get there, and how you're going to handle tasks at work and home while you're hobbled. It's very difficult to get through life without ever needing physical or mental health attention. Be sure that you know where to find that support when you need it.

Personal Support

This is where you are going to be doing the majority of the identification of your support system. Think back to when you made your diagram about the circles of people around you. Chances are good that the people who are in the smallest circles are the people who make up your personal support system. These are your family and friends and most trusted colleagues. If something exciting happens, who is the first person you tell? Good news, bad news, we all have someone that we *need* to talk to about it. For many people, this is a parent or sibling, a romantic partner, or a best friend. These are also the people who consider us to be part of their support system, as well. And that's how a healthy interpersonal relationship should be, with a mutual sense of closeness.

When we're children and haven't reached emotional maturity, we rely on our school friends to be our support system. These friendships can blossom into lifelong relationships, or they can die of attrition as we grow into ourselves and move into different phases of our lives. That doesn't take away any of the value of these early connections. Healthy childhood friendships, whether they last a year, a decade, or for life, form the foundation of the friendships we make as we go through the years.

As we age, we form new friendships based on mutual interests, personality compatibility, and shared experiences. The friendships we form as teenagers and adults teach us a lot about who we are at that stage in life and guide our emotional growth. It's important to note that it's not always the length of a friendship that makes it significant, but the depth. You may have a friend you've known since kindergarten and a friend you met in college, but the college friend may be a closer connection. That's okay. It's perfectly fine to have 'levels' of friendship that are based on closeness and not longevity. We rely on different people in our lives for different things.

Sibling relationships are also a good foundation for your support system. Although it can seem as if you and your siblings are at war when you are children, they are the people who have shared all your childhood experiences and will know what you are thinking and feeling, even when you don't even know yourself sometimes. Some people without siblings have similar relationships with cousins who are close in age.

A solid relationship with parents, grandparents, aunts, and uncles can also teach you a lot about healthy interactions. If you are lucky enough to grow up in a family with mutual respect and a nurturing environment, then you will have a good sense of how relationships should work from a young age. As you mature, you can pass that relationship respect onto your own children, nieces, nephews, and grandchildren. Of course, not all families are the most nurturing, and at worst can be extremely damaging, but we'll talk about that when we get to the section on cutting unhealthy relationships from your life.

Another source of personal support is from your significant other or romantic partner. Ideally, you are with your partner because you are emotionally compatible, meaning that you have the same relationship goals and are willing to work to ensure each other's happiness. There's a lot to be said about being able to tell your significant other everything that's going on in your life without feeling as if you'll be facing judgment. Our romantic partners should be a safe space, and although there's no guarantee that you'll never argue or have a disagreement, you should feel like it's still safe to have those conversations. An argument shouldn't involve personal attacks or make you feel belittled. This goes for disagreements with friends and family, too.

Spiritual Support

Before your mind jumps immediately to religion, that's not exactly what we mean here, although it can include organized worship. What we mean when we say spiritual support is finding something or someone that makes you feel good about yourself and your life. This could be yoga or kickboxing. This could be a religion or faith-based activity, like attending and participating in your church. It could be hiking or running. Your spirit is what makes you tick. You need to feed your spirit to keep your mind and your body happy. Your spiritual support person might be your athletic mentor or your clergy member. It's all about what's best for you. This is just a reminder that no matter how busy or stressful your life is, you need to find something to sustain you. Whether that is going to church or temple, or going rock-climbing, remember to find your spiritual support somewhere. It will be something that sustains you through tough times, even if it's planning a trip that may be far in the future- it's something to look forward to. Coordinating an event at your church may bring you closer to your community and make you feel good about giving back. There are endless ways to find spiritual support, so find what works for you and nurture that relationship between yourself, your spirit, and your everyday life.

Finding New Sources of Support

There are going to be times in everyone's life when they feel completely alone. Perhaps you have no family, at least not nearby, or you've moved to a new city and a new job and haven't found any friends yet. There are numerous reasons, whether by choice or circumstance, that a person might find themselves without a support system. If you find yourself in that position, what's the best way to begin building a new one or adding to an existing one?

The first thing you should do is to consider what you already have. If you've relocated for a new job, how are your coworkers? If they seem to be great, then you've probably already got professional support. Work on building those relationships to strengthen your mutual respect. Be sure to follow everything you've learned so far about setting boundaries. Being the new person at a workplace doesn't mean you need to be a doormat to get your colleagues to like you! Remember to be kind but firm, and you will quickly earn a reputation for being someone who treats their coworkers with compassion but also stands their ground.

The next support system we had on our list above was medical support. Even if you are someone who enjoys good health, you're going to need preventative care, like a general practitioner and dentist. One thing we hadn't mentioned, but that also bears a bit of weight, is also finding good medical support in a reputable veterinarian for your pets. If you've got medical insurance for yourself (and/or your pets), a great place to start your search is to look at the providers' lists on the insurance websites. You can also ask your old doctor(s) who they would recommend in your new city.

You should also make sure you look at reviews, both the good ones and the bad ones! Bad reviews can actually tell you a lot more about a business than good ones, especially once you weed out the ones obviously left by people who are picking bones for ridiculous reasons. If you see a handful of bad reviews all pointing towards the same problem, chances are good that their concerns are real.

Once you've found a general practitioner for yourself, make an appointment to meet them in person, and have your records transferred from your old provider. Introduce yourself, have a physical, or just sit and chat about your medical history. Establishing a relationship with a new provider when you're not sick will be tremendously helpful when you are in need of care.

If you have special medical needs or a chronic condition, and you find yourself in a situation where you need to build a new medical team, getting recommendations from your previous providers may be your best option. Learn where your closest hospital and/or trauma center is should you need immediate care. Again, look at reviews and try to determine the best options for you. Reading the opinions of other patients will let you know what type of care you can expect to receive. Make sure all your records, even if they are voluminous, are transferred to the proper offices, and set appointments to meet with the providers before you require acute care.

One other thing to consider when finding new medical support is transportation. If you drive, you'll probably be okay. But if you don't drive or if you were sick or injured and couldn't drive, is there public transportation readily available for you to get to your doctors' offices or the hospital? You should check for bus and train routes in your new city and determine if there are any non-service areas you should be aware of. If so, you can check for taxi and ambulette services and in lieu of those being available, check for local ride-sharing services like Lyft or Uber.

Personal and spiritual support are going to be the big things you need when you're building a new support system or adding to your existing one. These are so important to overall mental and physical well-being! Finding people who you trust and have mutual respect for is a crucial part of life, and it's always about quality, not quantity. One true friend is worth a thousand false friends. Do not allow people to walk all over you in the pursuit of friendship! Remember your boundaries and positive self-talk, and don't feel the need to change just to make someone like you. If you think you need to change, for any reason, make that decision by and for yourself, not to appease another person in return for friendship.

So, how do adults make new friends? It's so much easier for younger people- they meet new people all the time at school and through extracurricular activities. As we age, leave our school and college years behind, and move into the workplace, we do tend to meet fewer and fewer people. Thankfully, the internet age has removed a great deal of isolation and provides a tremendous source for research and finding like-minded people. The best place to start making new friends is by finding out where to practice your hobbies or finding organizations or clubs to join.

Search around your area for a place of worship that fits your needs or for clubs and groups that match up with your hobbies. The local library system is a great place to start, as these institutions usually host groups of diverse ages and interests- book clubs, yoga classes, crafting groups, movie lovers' clubs- you name it, libraries offer it these days. Libraries are also great resources for young families to meet other young families through story-times and parent/child classes.

Volunteering is also a terrific way to meet like-minded people and make new friends and connections. If you love animals, shelters are always looking for volunteers for all sorts of roles, from animal care through clerical work and transportation. You could find a non-profit group in your area that serves a population that you wish to help- homeless veterans, young families, children. These groups always need dedicated people with similar views to help them fill their budget gaps with volunteer work. You could also see if your municipality has any openings on their community boards; joining your town's recreation or environmental committee is a great way to meet your neighbors and give back while exploring your interests.

What if you're not a very extroverted person? Online communities are great, too! There are groups and clubs online that fit any interest, hobby, or budget! Many people find that they make new, fast, lifelong friends playing video games, learning a new skill, or joining an interest group online or through social media. For people with generalized or social anxiety or depression, or for people who have physical limitations, having friends online is a great way to stay connected to the world and find people with similar interests to 'hang out' with. The important thing is to find people who shore up your sense of self and with whom you can share your thoughts and feelings.

Saying Good-bye to Energy Vampires

As important as it is to find and keep people around you who make you feel good, that you have mutual respect for, and that are supportive and honest, it's also crucial to rid your life of anyone who doesn't fit that category. While it's difficult to avoid every single person who could possibly give you grief, you can make sure not to have them in your inner circle or let them bother you. We call these people 'energy vampires' because they seem to suck the spirit right out of you when you're around them.

Let's start with the hard one, and that's your family. Not all families are perfect. In fact, there is no such thing as a perfect family, but there are families who are loving and supportive, and there are families that are not. Just because you share a last name or a blood connection with someone, does not give them the right to treat you with anything less than respect. This can be tough to wrangle with, emotionally, especially if you grew up with parents who constantly belittled or abused you because no child wants to have to admit that their parents aren't the good guys. The same goes for siblings. These emotional wounds can be hard to heal, but it is possible.

This is where boundaries come into play, and the ability to draw behavioral lines for yourself can be the difference between feeling drained and feeling in control. Let's use a mother-daughter relationship as an example. Let's say that Mom is overbearing and attention-seeking, and calls the daughter selfish for wanting to strike out on her own and get her own place to live. The mother will likely be dramatic and try to guilt the daughter into staying, bemoaning how her child could leave her alone, and isn't the daughter grateful for having a mother who is willing to have her at home? The daughter can react as follows:

- Stay home and give up her dreams of being independent to appease her mother, thereby giving the mother more power and making herself miserable

     or

- Move out as planned, tell her mother she'll visit once a week, taking back control of her own life and setting a boundary with her mother

     or

- Move out as planned and cut her mother off completely, assuring that she won't be subject to another guilt trip ever again (at least not directly from mom)

The third option seems a bit extreme, but if this were real life and not an example, we might be inclined to agree with this course of action given other background information. The first option is what we want to avoid.

Being mentally tough and resilient means being able to make tough decisions, even when it comes to family. That means being confident in yourself, knowing your worth, and having the capability of setting those boundaries and sticking to them. If you are sticking to boundaries and the other person isn't, then you can move to 'no contact' and cut them out of your life. This isn't always going to be easy, but you have to do what's right for you and your mental health.

With the tough discussion about family out of the way, what do you do if you've got romantic relationships, friendships, or workplace connections that aren't going so well? Again, it's all about self-respect and boundaries. It can be hard to admit when a romantic relationship is coming to an end because sometimes, we give it our all, and it just isn't enough. Sometimes, the relationship is abusive, and it's hard to get out due to fear or lack of self-esteem. Being tough means finding the strength to say, "I can do this. I don't deserve this abuse. I'm getting out."

If you are in an abusive relationship and don't have an immediate support system that can help you find an escape route, you can visit www.thehotline.org, which includes a safety net- the back button reroutes users to a search engine page and blocks re-entry via using the back button again. They also have a 24-hour phone line in the United States at 1-800-799-7233. There is also a texting option, at 1-866-331-9474, by simply sending the phrase 'LoveIs' to that number to be connected with assistance.

When it comes to friendships, there should always be a balance of give and take. We've all had relationships that don't feel quite right; we might feel like we're being used, or that we're doing all the work in a friendship. Even if someone is going through a really tough time and you are offering support, you should always be able to say that they would do the same for you. If you can't, it might be time to rethink the boundaries of the friendship. This can be a difficult thing to do, but it will make you feel better in the long run. Friends should lift us up and make us feel happy, they should be there as a shoulder to cry on when we need support, they should love and respect us for who we are, and they should offer gentle, honest, constructive criticism when we're not exhibiting our best qualities.

What if you want to pull back from a relationship that isn't serving us well, but we're stuck in a school or work environment with that person? This is where boundaries and communication will be your best tools. You want to be firm, but kind. Try not to argue or escalate an argument. Explain to the person that their behavior is upsetting you and that you would like them to work with you to fix things up, or else you will need to remove yourself from that person's circle. Put it on yourself, if you must, to frame the conversation in a way that is going to be the most beneficial to your mental health. Then stick by your words.

If you are in a situation where you can't 'escape' an energy vampire, do your best to limit contact. Stand by the boundaries you have set, and don't spend any more time with them than you must. There will likely be pushback, but don't let it get to you. It's hard to admit that a friendship or work relationship just isn't in your best interest, but you need to protect yourself and your emotional health. There's no need to be rude, just go about your business and treat that person with due respect. You will find that every interaction will become easier until you've established the 'new normal' for your relationship with them. Time does heal wounds, albeit slowly sometimes.

Energy vampires can be everywhere- home, work, school, and in our clubs and organizations. It's nearly impossible as an adult to avoid being in contact with at least one or more of them. Being able to recognize the red flags of an energy vampire can help you avoid getting in too deep with them by setting boundaries before a problem exists. Here are some classic red flags to look for before you become romantically, professionally, or emotionally involved with an energy vampire:

- Lack of accountability; nothing is ever their fault or their responsibility
- Lack of empathy; they cannot put themselves in another person's shoes
- Lack of sympathy; they take the feelings of others into account
- Lack of reciprocation; they take more from a relationship than they give back
- Need for attention; they create situations in which they are the main character
- Need for cruelty; they say inappropriate things for shock value and to cause pain
- Need for drama; they turn every scenario into a catastrophe, despite easy solutions
- Need to isolate; they want you to themselves and are jealous of other people in your life

Do any of these sound familiar to you? If so, you definitely have some energy vampires in your life. These behaviors can set you on edge and make you feel as if you have to walk on eggshells around these people. You have to try to appease them to keep the peace or just avoid the inevitable stream of complaints. Or do you? When you set healthy boundaries with energy vampires, you can expect some pushback. People who have been taking advantage of you for a while aren't going to be thrilled when you begin standing up for yourself. You'll likely become the subject of their complaints for a while.

You need to be prepared for this pushback but stand your ground. Don't let yourself be bullied into moving those boundaries back, or you'll find your psyche being conquered again. Even if others come to you asking about why you've changed your relationship with someone, you don't owe them an explanation, because the energy vampire's actions will speak for themselves, eventually. These things always come out in the wash.

If you're feeling uncomfortable because you're experiencing pushback or fallout from setting new boundaries with an energy vampire, it's okay. That's normal, and it's fine to be sad or angry over the loss or restructuring of an old relationship. Remember our traits of resilient people? This is an instance where you will use the need to recognize that nothing lasts forever. The acute discomfort or emotional pain you feel from changing the boundaries of a relationship will fade and heal with time.

Being able to ignore the negativity that comes with setting boundaries for an energy vampire is a great show of resiliency. Some of your energy vampires will get the picture, and the relationship will either improve, or it will find a neutral equilibrium. There will be some that cannot handle the new dynamic. You may have to go 'no contact' if you still don't feel comfortable with the way the relationship is heading. Remember, this is about how you feel and about your mental health. Even if you are stuck in a school or work setting with your energy vampire, you can be civil when you must and then avoid all unnecessary contact.

Take the time to allow yourself to heal from broken or adjusted relationships. Just because a relationship wasn't fulfilling to you doesn't mean you didn't put a lot of time and emotional energy into it, and you deserve to be able to grieve those relationships. It's okay to miss a friend even if they didn't always treat you very well. But if you are actively working toward building a healthy support system and eliminating or healing a broken one, you can feel confident that you are on your way to resiliency and the mental toughness you're seeking.

In the next chapter, we're going to talk about everything that can go wrong. Maybe that's a little dramatic, but we are going to be discussing what to do when things don't go your way. The best-laid plans can go awry, so how can you continue to build and maintain your mental toughness when life seems hellbent on knocking you down? That's the main concept we'll be examining in Chapter 5, so let's take a look.

CHAPTER 5
Bend, Don't Break

Life stinks. Love hurts. The best-laid plans of mice and men. Insert all the other clichés that mean that no matter what you've got planned for yourself and your future, something will get in the way. The truth is that life is unpredictable. Things do happen. How can we avoid getting derailed and getting mired in negativity? In other words, how do we continue to build and maintain resilience even in the face of unexpected setbacks? To dive into this subject, we'll have to go back and take another look at the traits of mentally tough people and how they apply to being able to use your resilience when life doesn't go as planned.

Self-Esteem and Boundaries

There are times when our self-esteem is going to take a hit. A romantic relationship ends out of the blue, or a project you'd poured your heart into isn't well-received. It hurts! It's okay to feel hurt; it's what happens after the hurt that defines your resilience. Sometimes, it's easy to brush things off with a simple "who cares, anyway?" Sometimes, things fester a little bit. Maybe somebody said something that stuck in your craw or that you just can't seem to shake off. The first thing you need to do is ask yourself why it is bothering you so much.

If someone has said something cruel to you, it can sting. It almost forces you into a loop of self-examination. What if you really *are* *whatever that person said about you*? Chances are good that you're not, but the problem with cruel things is that they chip away at even the best self-esteem and sow seeds of self-doubt. The remedy for that self-doubt is positive self-talk. Take what's been said to you and turn it on its head. If you've been called 'selfish,' remind yourself of all the things you do to exhibit selflessness. What would cause the person to say this to you? It was probably projection- using a negative feeling about themselves and attributing it to you instead. While it's not your job to psychoanalyze others, giving it some thought can help you understand why someone might say something cruel and untrue to you. It is a reflection on them, not on you. Remind yourself of your worth, and don't let your ego take too much of a hit. It's not worth your time.

But what if what they said was harsh but happened to be true? What if you acted with poor judgment and actually hurt someone? Or, worse, what if it wasn't a one-off and you do have an undesirable personality trait? It might be time for a change, and while the truth can hurt, it can lead to better things. Use their words as a learning experience. Don't blame anyone but yourself. Apologize if you need to, and do it sincerely. Then figure out a way to enact a personal change. It is possible. You can use what you've learned here already to apply it to make any personality change that you need to. Set a goal and be mindful of your behavior and the responses of others.

Boundaries are also an important part of recovering from a blow to your self-esteem. If you burned yourself on the stove, you wouldn't immediately put your hand back on the hot burner. You would step away from the stove, nurse your wound, and then be careful not to let it happen again. When someone hurts you with their words or actions, you should take the time to recover and then keep your distance; in other words, you need to set a new boundary. Setting boundaries with those who have hurt us is an act of resilience in and of itself. It shows that you have enough self-respect to say, "That's enough. You aren't going to hurt me again!"

What if it isn't a cruel remark that causes you pain, but the flop of a major endeavor? If you've put your all into a project or trained your hardest for a sporting event, only to have things not go as planned can be hurtful. It's difficult not to feel like a failure. It's what you do with your feelings that will indicate your mental toughness. Go ahead and grieve if your boss didn't like the presentation you spent hours of your best effort on creating. Cry if you tried your damnedest and didn't excel at your track meet. It's okay! It always bears repeating that being mentally tough doesn't mean being unfeeling.

If you feel that you've had a professional or personal failure, you must think critically about why. Try your best to be objective and come to reasonable conclusions. If you've been offered constructive criticism, take it. But if you examine the situation and you cannot find a single thing that you could have done differently, then you need to decide what the root of the problem was and how you can overcome it the next time. If it turns out that your boss just has it out for you or the track meet was rigged, then what's your course of action? Do you continue to push, or do you set boundaries? Or, alternately, do you walk away completely? The ability to make these decisions and stick by them is a hallmark of mental toughness.

Self-esteem and boundary-setting are lifelong learning processes. Every time our ego takes a hit, it's human nature to question the intent and accuracy of the words or events that caused our doubt. The truth is, even those people who always seem to be confident suffer from self-doubt. It's what they do with that self-doubt that defines their next moves and restores their confidence. We talked about analyzing cruel words. Yes, maybe you are doing something or have done something wrong, and you may need to make a change. It is more likely, though, you haven't done anything wrong.

Remembering that not one single person goes through life without feeling self-doubt at some point can help you feel a little less alone when you're feeling down on yourself. It's a shared human experience to have highs and lows of self-esteem. By keeping this in mind and continually working on your self-esteem and positive self-talk, you'll see that you'll be more consistently on the higher end of the self-esteem chart.

One last note about self-esteem and boundaries. You should never let anyone tell you that you don't deserve to feel good about yourself or have the self-worth to set positive boundaries. Many people who struggle or have struggled with low self-esteem are fearful of seeming cocky or selfish if they stand up for themselves. There's a huge difference between being cocky and being confident. You want to strive for confidence that says, "I got this; let me show you what I'm capable of." Confidence means you know what you can do, and you can back it up in word and action.

By contrast, cockiness says, "I'm the best; just take my word for it!" There is often no action to back up those words. When you are building your self-esteem with positive self-talk, you want to emphasize the skills that you can back up. It's okay to not be good at everything. Work on fundamentals and build your skills from there. With each new thing that you master, you'll see that your self-esteem increases along with it. Think about learning a technical skill like playing a musical instrument. You begin by learning the basics- things like finger placement and reading a staff. The next step is learning keys and scales. Then you learn basic songs and work your way towards proficiency in playing more difficult tunes. But even the most talented, skilled musicians in the world still practice their fundamentals regularly.

It is the same when you are working on shoring up your self-esteem and learning to set boundaries. Start with the fundamentals and build on your skills as you grow your ability to use positive self-talk and healthy boundaries. Remind yourself often that you are worthy of respect and act in a way that proves it. When you are confident in yourself and your abilities, you will carry yourself in a way that shows that confidence to others. It's a cycle, and if you want to be the type of person who is seen as resilient in the face of a personal or professional blow, you can use your confidence to recover. Once you've established your cycle of recovery, confidence, and resilience, it will be hard to break, even in the face of crisis.

This also goes for setting boundaries. It's difficult at first, and since this chapter is about emotional and mental flexibility, the key thing to remember about boundaries is that they can be changed, but only if you are comfortable with changing them and it's not to the detriment of your mental health. We talked earlier about setting boundaries by being firm but kind. You may find yourself in a scenario where you need or want to move an existing boundary. Perhaps someone who hurt you in the past, and whom you've been keeping at arm's length, is in a situation that they need dire assistance with, and you're the only person who can help them. What to do?

Being able to be compassionate while not compromising yourself is a good way to be flexible while still protecting your boundaries. You can explain that you're helping 'this time' but that the person is not to expect things to go back to your previous level of closeness. Then stick by that. Being able to bend your boundaries without breaking your word is important to your mental and emotional health. Life isn't always as easy as black and white, and being emotionally flexible enough to set and modify boundaries on a case-by-case basis will help you build mental toughness and learn your own emotional limits.

If we want to sum up the key points about self-esteem, boundaries, and being able to find flexibility, it's about being firm and finding your cycle. Practice makes perfect when it comes to building self-esteem. The harder you work at it, the more naturally it will come. Over time, you will find that you make boundary decisions more quickly and with stronger conviction, and that your self-esteem takes less of a blow whenever something doesn't go quite right.

Using Your Support System and Outlets

When you're hurting from an unexpected attack, a stressful event, or a perceived failure, one of the best ways you can maintain your resilience and make important decisions is to lean on your support system. This can provide you with feedback from trusted friends and family and give you the emotional boost you need to get through tough times. Try to be open and honest about the situation, no matter how hurt you are feeling. People can only lend objective advice when they are given all the facts.

Having a solid support system can give you a feeling of security and peace of mind. It's so hard to get through life completely alone, and when things are rough, having people you can rely on will make things a little brighter. Talking through issues that are bothering you gives you a sense of relief and clarity. Sometimes, when you say things aloud or type them into an email or text message, you'll have an epiphany. Being able to verbalize what you're feeling makes you think about it in a different way. We all know that internalizing your problems never makes for a good outcome. Sure, you may feel strong at the time- "Look at me not needing anyone! I'm fine!"- but in the long run, those feelings can boil over and come out in an unhealthy way.

When you've got a strong support system, you've got built-in cheerleaders, sympathetic ears, and people who will tell you, gently and honestly, when you need to rethink things. If you're feeling heartbroken or trying to make a big decision, having the perspective of others that you trust can be the difference between being stuck in a rut and taking positive action to improve your situation. Our support system is what gets us proper physical and mental health care, works with us to get through tough times in our careers, and acts as a sounding board and soft place to land when life doesn't go quite to plan, or we suffer a traumatic event.

It's also important to think about your healthy outlets when life deals you a bad hand. Like we said, bottling up negative emotions isn't healthy. There are some that might look down on you for pursuing your hobby when the world's gone to hell, but too bad. You know what's best for you, and if a round of golf with your buddies a few days after your parent's funeral is going to be good for you, then, by all means, tee off! If you're a runner, run. If you're a knitter, make the world's longest scarf. It's okay to use your healthy outlets as a way to blow off steam or move away from your troubles for a while. That's why they are called healthy outlets!

Try to avoid falling into a pattern of unhealthy or self-destructive behaviors. Did your fiancé leave you? Okay, maybe you get a free pass on a weekend bender, but don't make a habit of that. Ride out your hangover and lean on your support system. They are the ones that will help you heal and get your life back together. Ask your friends if you can plan something fun. Talk to them about what's going on in your life and why you need some time with them. Don't force an uneasy conversation, but you'd be surprised how much talking you can do while taking a nice hike or playing a round of golf. You'll feel better, even if you can't come up with an easy solution to your problem.

Leaning on your support system and expressing yourself through healthy outlets will help you begin to heal, even if it doesn't feel like it right away. If you are grieving for a lost loved one, the end of a relationship, or a professional setback, you should know that grief in any form takes time to work through. Sometimes, grief never goes away but becomes a dull ache rather than a sharp pain. Use the resources available to you in your support system and your hobbies to work through the grief, hurt, and anger you are feeling, and you'll find that it's a lot easier than bottling things up and going it alone.

As the old cliché says, time heals all wounds. Not feeling alone can help the healing process, and using your healthy outlets will take your mind off things, give you mental space to process what's hurting you, and may be the distraction you need to have an 'aha!' moment. While time *does* heal, the deeper the wound, the more likely they are to leave a scar. No one would ever suggest that you can or should forget something that hurt you deeply but allowing yourself to lean on your support system and giving yourself the freedom to participate in your healthy outlets will at least stop you from picking at the emotional scab, which will lengthen the healing process and leave a bigger scar.

Maintaining Mindfulness and Embracing the Present

There's a phrase that's frequently used in the military called 'embracing the suck.' Embracing the suck means that no matter how bad things seem, if you can't do anything about it, you just have to ride it out. This ties back into our concept that resilient people recognize that nothing is forever. That awareness of the impermanence of stress and pain is such a vital part of building and maintaining mental toughness.

There will be times when a situation is unsolvable. Some things just are what they are, until they aren't anymore. It's a fact of life, and while it can be painful to deal with at the moment, you can remind yourself that the situation won't be forever, the pain will fade, and you will be okay again. Being a mindful person can help you get through having to 'embrace the suck.' When you are cognizant of the situation, present in the moment, and aware of the feelings and reactions of others around you, you'll be better equipped to handle whatever it is you're dealing with.

No matter how tough things get, using your everyday mindfulness exercises and grounding techniques can get you through even the most stressful of moments. Remember to breathe and find your center. Life's not easy. Even the most privileged of people have tough times. You never have to feel ashamed of feeling stressed or overwhelmed. You can be wealthy and be dealing with poor emotional health. You can be homeless and happy as a clam. Your story is unique to YOU! Live in your reality and make the best of it as you can. Being mentally tough means realizing that you are in control and that the decisions you make will be the ones that dictate where your life is heading.

When we're talking about applying mindfulness and being present in the moment, flexibility without compromise is just as important as it is to self-esteem and boundaries. Being grounded and dialed into what is going on around you allows you to make both practical and emotional decisions on the fly and be comfortable with those decisions. Having a grasp on any situation and being able to move quickly and decisively is a good sign that you are on your way to resiliency because it shows that you have the emotional strength to handle decision-making and any potential fallout from a poor decision.

Learning and Moving On

So, what if you make a bad decision? We all have. It's what we do after it becomes apparent that defines your resiliency. Consider your options carefully. Think about the decision, the consequences, and what choices you have to make to rectify the situation and move on. Using the phrase 'bad decision' is painting life with a broad brush, though. You can decide to paint your living room and then hate the color when you've finished. Is it the end of the world? No, it's an inconvenience that can be remedied with another afternoon's work and a fresh supply of paint.

There are also the kinds of decisions that can be life-altering. Driving drunk and causing an accident. Hurting a romantic partner or beloved family member with inappropriate actions. Cheating on an important exam. Life is full of terrible choices just waiting to be made! These are just some examples of what not to do because these might be unrecoverable mistakes. If you are lucky enough to have the choice to make good on some of these mistakes, you should take the chance and learn from what you've done, make amends where you can, and accept the fact that people may never see you the same way again.

The sorts of decisions we are most concerned with here in this book are the kind of decisions you need to make in everyday work and home life, and learning not to let mistakes derail your emotional and mental health. Being resilient means that one piece of constructive criticism from a work supervisor isn't going to ruin your whole week. It means that a minor argument with your partner isn't going to mess with your head so badly you don't know what to do. Resilient people know how to compromise, learn from their errors, and move ahead with purpose.

Some people are simply wired to be more sensitive than others, but that doesn't mean that sensitive people can't also be mentally tough. Yes, being resilient can mean, in part, being thick-skinned, but you don't have to be a rhino- you could also be a duck and let things roll off your back. There are a lot of ways to show your resilience without compromising your emotional side. It's brilliant to be an emotional person, but it's also okay to be more of a calculated thinker. Some people are passionate, and some are stoic, but all people can learn to embrace their personality, admit where they've erred and need to improve, and be flexible enough with the people around them to do so.

When you've made a decision that has a poor outcome, the first step to bouncing back is to admit it. Take responsibility for your actions and if you've hurt someone, apologize. Then analyze what went wrong, and make amends. If it can't be fixed, then you need to figure out how not to let it happen again. Compromise on your actions if you need to, but remember not to compromise your self-esteem or your boundaries. It is possible to do this, we promise. You can admit a mistake and find a way to rectify it without permanent damage to your self-esteem or your values.

There is a certain kind of power that comes from holding yourself accountable for a mistake. It keeps the ball in your court and gives you more freedom to decide what happens next. While you may have caused hurt or discord at home or in the workplace, you have a much better chance of being respected and forgiven if you admit a mistake and apologize before someone asks you to. It shows that you value the people around you. When the dust settles, you will still be able to hold your head high because you made it through and took responsibility for yourself- which is another sign of growing and maintaining resiliency.

Using personal accountability in conjunction with positive self-talk and mindfulness is a good way to develop the emotional flexibility you need to maintain resilience. After all, resilience doesn't exist without the ability to change and adapt, and that is what keeps us moving forward, growing, and thriving as we navigate this crazy world. As we head into the last chapter, we want you to keep thinking about those common traits of resilient people. We're going to finish up our exploration of mental toughness by looking at long-term strategies you can use to build and maintain a resilient life.

CHAPTER 6
Tough For Life

We've spent the whole book talking about building and maintaining mental toughness, and hopefully, by now, you've decided that the journey to resiliency is worth the hard mental and emotional work. In this last chapter, we're going to talk about the long-term things you can do to stay resilient for life. It's always the hard work that needs doing first, but if you've done a solid job of living up to and emulating the traits of naturally resilient people, then you're ready for maintenance tips and techniques to keep you tough for life.

Mindfulness and Meditation

Earlier, we talked about brief mindfulness exercises that you can use to alleviate sudden stress, clear your mind, and ground yourself when you experience anxiety. Here, we're going to talk more about mindfulness techniques that you can use for meditative purposes to further your resiliency journey. When you take time to reflect and be present in your own reality, you will be more attuned to the world around you at any given time. Being more aware allows you to see problems before they arise, by reading the moods of those around you, sensing tension before it can escalate, and finding solutions to defuse stressful situations with intentional calm.

One way to fit meditative mindfulness techniques into your life is to mark aside a little bit of time every day for this purpose. This can be something you do in the morning before you start your 'get ready' routine or in the evening when you're winding down for bed. You could even practice some meditation during the day if you've got a long enough lunch break. Let's take a look at some daily mindfulness exercises and meditation techniques that you can use to live a life of emotional balance.

* **The White Light**- Sitting down comfortably, close your eyes and imagine that you are being suspended by a string at the very top of your head. This will immediately make you improve your posture, which increases blood flow and oxygenation. Take a few deep breaths, in through your nose, pause, out through your mouth. When you are settled, and your breathing is regulated, you're going to imagine a white light moving down the invisible string above your head. Picture the light coming slowly down over your head, bathing you in calm.

Now imagine that the light is moving down your entire body, over your shoulders, arms, and torso, down through your core, your legs, and all the way down to your toes. Let the light move slowly, and imagine the calm and warmth it is bringing to your extremities. Once you've imagined your entire body encompassed by this white light, slowly picture it receding, back up your legs, your trunk, your upper body, and finally your

46

head. The light then floats off and disappears. When you've completed this exercise, you should feel calm and in tune with your body and your senses.

* The Internal Checklist- In this exercise, which is similar to a Corpse Pose in hatha yoga, you're going to lay on your back, arms loosely at your sides, legs slightly apart. Take a few deep breaths (again, in through the nose, pause, out through the mouth) and let yourself relax. Imagine that all the stress in your body is sinking out the bottom and into the ground below you. Picture all your tension seeping out of your cells and oozing away forever. Now, do a body check. Wiggle your toes and concentrate on how your feet feel. Move up and deliberately think about your shins and calves, your knees, your thighs, and so on, up through your hips, back, and torso, down your arms (wiggle those fingers) and your shoulders, neck, and head.

You want to think about each body part. Does it hurt? Does it feel good today? If you've got pain or discomfort, what is causing it? Is it fixable? Was it related to your stress and tension? These are the things you should ask yourself. Focus on how your clothes feel against your skin and how it feels to wiggle your toes inside your socks. These are the tiny sensations you want to train your brain to concentrate on because self-awareness will help you build situational awareness. This is a great exercise to do before going to bed since it involves such a deep focus on relaxation and awareness.

* The To-do List- This is a wonderful exercise to get your day started on the right foot, and it only takes a few minutes. When you get up in the morning, set aside a little time to think about your intentions for the day. Sit quietly and close your eyes. Picture yourself getting ready for work or school, and mentally walk through all the things you want to accomplish with your day. Even if you're a stay-at-home parent or you're looking for new work, you can map out your daily to-do list in your mind.

Concentrate on picturing yourself completing your tasks. Think about the realistic amount of time these tasks will take you. Feel the satisfaction of getting them done, but also think about the consequences of not finishing them- not to stress yourself out, but to help you realize what your priorities should be. Which tasks carry more weight? Which are lower on the list and could potentially be postponed if things don't go right? This helps you mentally prepare yourself to deal with unexpected interruptions or roadblocks. When you've finished your mental walkthrough, you'll be more ready to handle your daily business with purpose and calm.

* The Mind Map- This exercise is a great way to find your 'happy place' and work towards your goals, whether they are related to finding resiliency or any other aspect of your life. Mind-mapping is useful for exploring possibilities, seeking calm, and keeping perspective on your goals and readjusting if necessary. You can do this exercise anywhere, just sit comfortably and close your eyes. Take a few deep breaths to calm yourself, and imagine a path.

Your path can be anything you want it to be. A city sidewalk, a quiet woodland trail, or a canal or stream with a boat to take you on your journey- anything you like! It's your mental map. At the end of this path is going to be your goals. Take yourself along this path. Picture each part of your journey as a step towards the goal. What should you be doing to attain what you want? Think of it almost as a choose-your-own-adventure book. If you walk a certain way, where will you end up? Is it where you want to be, and if not, what alternate action should you take? You can also erect a metal building that gives yourself a sense of calm. Perhaps it's a rustic cabin. Maybe it's a dusty old honky-tonk bar where you picture yourself having a cold beer and watching the dancing. Think about what makes you feel calm and happy, and create an internal space where you experience that safety and peace. Give yourself time and practice to become comfortable with both mapping a mental path and visualizing a mental happy place. The more you visit these places in your mind, the easier they will become to recall and visit. Create a world for yourself where you feel unhurried and can explore your feelings and your goals. You want to feel deliberate and purposeful as you go from Point A to Point B, C, D, and beyond.

* The Mental Model- Mental modeling is a technique that is most often associated with a field of study known as neuro linguistic programming or NLP. This field is dismissed by some as a pseudoscience, but there are visualization elements that are useful for everyday meditation and mindfulness. One of these exercises is mental modeling. It's similar to mind mapping, in that you will be picturing reaching a goal, but there are a couple of distinct differences. In NLP-style mental modeling, you won't be focused solely on your own path, but also on the path of someone you admire and wish to emulate, or 'model.' You want to imagine what it took for them to achieve the quality or qualities you admire and find a way to either emulate or learn from their path. The main concept behind this exercise is that if it's worked for someone else, then it's a proven path, and you should also be able to follow it.

Take time to examine why you admire this person. Since we are talking about mental toughness and resilience, then this is obviously someone whose strength you respect. Perhaps it's a personal acquaintance or friend. Maybe it's an athlete or other celebrity who overcame a challenge to achieve their goals. Be specific about what it is you admire and would like to emulate. Is it the way they handle medical treatment without complaint? Perhaps they fought their way from a traumatic childhood to attain personal and professional success in adulthood. If you really want to know who someone is and what makes them tick so that you can emulate them, learn everything you can about them. Don't be a stalker, of course, but look at their social media and see what their values seem to be. Read biographies or talk to people that know them personally. You may find that your admiration grows, or you might find that you no longer want to emulate that person. Either way, you have learned something about them and about yourself.

When you practice mental modeling, you'll want to take time to sit comfortably and relax. Close your eyes and take a few cleansing breaths. Picture the person you want to model performing the action or expressing the emotion you admire them for. Think about what they might be feeling or thinking while they do it. Try to put yourself into the head of that person. Lastly, picture yourself doing and feeling these same things- handling a situation with calm and poise or using your mental strength to get past a stressful, emotional hurdle. When you can consistently place yourself in that spot and mentally achieve your goals, then you are ready to achieve them in the real world.

* **Mantras for All Occasions**- We talked earlier about using mantras back in Chapter 3 when we talked about setting goals, writing mission statements, and drawing pep talks out from those statements. Mantras are a great way to keep you in touch with reality and instantly change your mood, and so we thought it might be a good idea to expand on the concept and show you how to use mantras in different ways, including for meditation.

Mantras are designed to reset your brain and make you focus on one important idea or reminder. You can use a mantra that is a snippet from a goal statement, like we discussed earlier, as a pep talk when hit with a sudden stressful situation, or you can use a longer mantra as a concept for meditation, to help you gain self-awareness, concentrate on a goal, or work through a difficult decision. When you meditate on a mantra, try to choose something that is specific and goal-oriented. This will help you find focus. One of the most difficult things about meditation is to not let your mind wander, and making sure your mantra is specific will help you keep on track.

We've talked about a lot of the facets of mentally tough people, and you can use mantras to meditate on any of these traits. You can boost your self-esteem with mantras that point out your positive qualities. This is a great way to use positive self-talk. You can also create mantras for meditation that revolve around your resilience goals, or mantras that offer gratitude for your support system. Think of mantras as your personal propaganda campaign. The more you hear and think about things, the more you will begin to believe them.

When you meditate, try to sit still and maintain good posture. You could find a comfortable chair, or sit cross-legged on the floor or a bed. Before you begin concentrating on your mantra, try to free your mind of all other things. Make a conscious effort to release tension, and take a few deep breaths to cleanse your system. Close your eyes and recite your mantra. You can do this aloud or internally. Focus on what each word means to you. Think about nothing else but your mantra, reciting it slowly and repetitively until you can 'feel' the words.

As you evolve and move towards achieving your goals, adjust your mantras. Use them to reflect the personal change you've undertaken and the change that's yet to come. Use mantras to instigate an 'aha!' moment by ruminating on your options for solving a problem or making a major decision. Meditation time is your time, and you can make the most out of it by focusing on the things that are on your mind while you're in a relaxed state away from immediate stress.

The more you practice your meditation and mindfulness techniques, the more adept you will be at understanding what your brain needs to function with poise, resilience, and grace in nearly every situation. In a later segment, we'll tie this concept together with our next topic, which is all about acceptance and forgiveness. As we come to the end of our time together, you should be seeing how it all fits in the big picture of mental toughness, and you should have a good idea by now of what your goals are going to be and how you can choose which methods you've learned here to best achieve those goals. Let's get into the homestretch.

Finding Forgiveness and Acceptance

No matter how hard you work at changing your life to be more resilient, there are always going to be things that you cannot change. Whether you are a religious person or not, you've probably run across the Serenity Prayer at some point in your life. To refresh your memory, it reads:

Grant me the serenity to accept the things I cannot change,
The courage to change the things I can,
And the wisdom to know the difference.

These are some solid concepts, and it sums up what we'll be talking about in this section. We've spent the entire book talking about and teaching you how to change things. But what happens when you come up against a roadblock that can't be moved or gotten around? What happens when something catastrophic forces you to admit an unrecoverable loss? Maybe it's when you're faced with these scenarios that you will find the true depth of your resiliency. Sadly, that can often be the case. We don't know how much we can handle until our limits are tested.

There's a branch of cognitive-behavioral therapy that's known as acceptance and commitment therapy, and this behavioral method focuses on being able to move forward from things we cannot change and commit to behaving in an acceptable manner. There are three tenets of acceptance and commitment therapy, and they are designated with the apt acronym ACT:

A- **Accept** the immovable facts of a situation
C- **Choose** the appropriate response to those facts
T- **Take** action to follow through with your response

What this acronym tells us is to slow down and be deliberate about our responses. When you use the ACT method to work through a personal crisis or negative scenario, you have to take time and be accountable for yourself. You have to choose the appropriate response. Think about it like this: You've gone to your favorite restaurant, and you're looking forward to having their signature dish. You sit down, order your drinks, and an appetizer, but when it comes time to request your entrée, the server tells you they've run out! Hit the pause button. What are your potential courses of action given that you CANNOT change the fact that the restaurant is out of stock, which is the immovable fact? You could:

1) Blow up because this is unacceptable! You could throw a tantrum that your favorite dish isn't available today, likely embarrassing yourself, your date, and the restaurant staff. You storm out. Now you'll probably be ashamed to or disallowed to come back, and you've lost your go-to dinner spot over not getting the prime rib.

2) Tell the server it's okay, order something else for dinner, and promise yourself that you'll get that favorite entrée next time. Make a mental note to come earlier when you next want to eat at this restaurant, and when you call to make your reservation, ask about the dish's availability that day.

3) Tell the server that you understand it's not their fault, but you won't be staying. Be sure to pay and tip for your drinks and appetizers, and go someplace else to eat. You haven't burned bridges, but you've expressed your displeasure by taking your business elsewhere for the evening.

In the first example, the whole idea of ACT has been thrown out the window. You couldn't find a way to accept that the restaurant was out of your favorite dish, and you've acted inappropriately and out of proportion to the situation. If you don't have prime rib tonight, what is the long-term consequence? There is none. You simply didn't have prime rib, and yet you've lost your cool and let it define your whole evening, and perhaps been labeled as a problem customer. Therefore, your lack of prime rib may not have direct lasting consequences, but your actions do. In the second example, we see acceptance. You have accepted that there is no prime rib at the restaurant, and you have chosen to stay and eat something else. You know that your best course of action is to remind yourself to make an earlier reservation next time. You still have a pleasant evening, and there are no long-term negative repercussions from your dining experience. You accepted the facts, you chose an appropriate response, and you've laid out a course of action for next time.

In the third example, we see an alternate course of action that also follows with ACT. You're accepting of the fact that you won't be getting the dish you came for, and you choose an appropriate and proportionate course of action. It may not have been the most graceful, but it was decisive and will have no long-term consequences.

That's the whole concept of ACT. It's designed to help you think before you do something inappropriate. It also focuses on not catastrophizing things. Remember when we talked about mountains and molehills? You can think about that when you think about acceptance. Ask yourself if your reaction is equal to the stimuli, and hold yourself accountable for your feelings. While there are always going to be things in life that we cannot change, what we can change is how we react and respond to them. Even in times of intense anger or intense grief, we can take a lesson from ACT and apply it towards our behaviors.

Acceptance places the burden solely onto our own shoulders. When there is nothing to be done, no solutions to be found, and no course of action other than to accept an unfortunate circumstance, the only thing left to control is our response. If you're dealing with the loss of a loved one, you must find a way to work through the stages of grief, the last of which is acceptance. Grief is a raw, dirty emotion. It can make us feel stripped of our humanity and lead us down unhealthy mental paths. If you can overcome grief and get to the acceptance phase, you can count yourself among the resilient.

Grief over the loss of a loved one isn't the only scenario in which we need to find acceptance. You may be on the losing end of a romantic breakup or the estrangement of a family relationship. Perhaps someone you love is going through a tough time, and you're unable to assist them. We can even get thrown off-course by unchangeable events at work or in our social lives. The key thing that you must remember is that your reaction is yours alone. You must choose how you are going to respond to negative stimuli. Being able to react appropriately and take responsibility for your reaction is the difference between resilience and breakdown. Remember what you've learned about mountains and molehills and apply that knowledge to scenarios that require acceptance.

Forgiveness is another chapter of the same story. We've all heard the phrase 'forgive and forget.' If only it was that simple! How we forgive people and even if we forgive people depends an awful lot on the person, the relationship, and the offense. The resilience in forgiveness comes from having the self-worth to set boundaries and say, "You won't hurt me again." Forgiveness is a funny thing, and sometimes its true meaning can get muddied. Forgiveness doesn't mean that a relationship immediately reverts to its previous state, nor does it automatically erase the hurt that was caused.

No, forgiveness means that you have searched your heart and your emotions and realized that it is not in your best interest to hold onto hate or bear a grudge. In some circumstances, you may wait forever for an apology that never comes, and it's up to you to heal without ever hearing an 'I'm sorry.' This is painful, but if someone doesn't see a problem with their painful actions, then it's on you to set the boundary, nurse your wounds, and not let them close enough to do it again. When someone truly cannot see how they've hurt you, you are better off without them. Grieve the relationship, resolve to hold firm on your boundaries, and let yourself heal. Holding hate towards them won't affect them at all, but it will negatively affect you. Don't let it. Use what you've learned about positive self-talk and building self-esteem to move past the pain and continue towards your goals.

Sometimes it's very easy to forgive someone. We get irritated with a child who draws on a wall, but we don't stay mad for very long. And we've all dealt with a friend or family member that's acted out of character and deserves a second chance. We wouldn't be able to get through this life without the ability to forgive the people that we love and receiving forgiveness in return. It's what we do with that ability that defines our mental toughness, teaches others that we respect them and require respect in return, and indicates that we're still capable of showing love even while we set boundaries to protect ourselves.

One of the things we often get angry about when we've been wronged is that we think that someone 'should have known better.' When it comes to the wrongdoings of a child, that's why it's easier to forgive. Your toddler drew on the wall, but they probably didn't know better, until you teach them. You correct the behavior, you teach the lesson, you forgive them, and move on. When it's the behavior of another adult, it becomes more of a gray area. It's easier to forgive when you believe that the offense was unintentional or an honest mistake.

When you've been intentionally wronged, it's harder to forgive, but it's also easier to set the necessary emotional boundaries. It goes back to self-preservation if you remember our hot stove analogy from earlier. When you're hurt, you're going to be quicker to distance yourself from the person or thing that hurt you. While there are always going to be instances where someone deserves a second chance, judge those occurrences on a case-by-case basis. Use your positive self-talk and meditation techniques to work through the issue. Only you can decide where to draw the line between being forgiving and preserving your mental and emotional health. You are not obligated to forgive anyone who you don't believe deserves your forgiveness, and you're also not obligated to explain yourself to anyone who questions why.

That's a key theme of both acceptance and forgiveness. They are intensely personal processes, and how you handle them belongs to no one else but you. While that means you don't owe anyone an explanation, that also means that you must take responsibility for your actions and behaviors. This is a vital part of being able to say that you conducted yourself with resiliency.

What we haven't talked about yet on these topics is the ability to accept and forgive *yourself*. You can draw boundaries and grieve the loss of relationships with other people, but what happens when you need to reflect upon forgiving yourself or accepting something about yourself that you cannot change? Let's focus on self-acceptance for a few moments.

There are times in everyone's life where they feel a bit of self-loathing. The early teenage years certainly spring to mind; this is a time where you're really finding out who you are and what your interests are. You're making new friends and exploring your personality, sexuality, and where you fit into your family dynamic as you mature. Anytime that we, as humans, are experiencing a period of growth or change, it opens us up to self-doubt and self-loathing. Like everything else we've talked about here, it comes down to accountability and positive self-improvement.

When you're feeling down on yourself, either in general or in response to a specific incident, it's time to double down on your positive self-talk. Use the skills you've learned throughout this book to determine the extent of the issue and employ your critical thinking and goal-setting skills. Rely on your mindfulness exercises to help you be present in the problem and find calm to work out solutions. If you determine that you can find room for self-improvement, use your mental toughness skills to achieve that goal. If you find that you've made a mountain out of a molehill, just be mindful not to let your perceived infraction happen again. Don't beat yourself up- move on.

But what if you *have* really done it? WE ALL MAKE MISTAKES! It is what happens after that mistake is made that defines not only our resiliency but our personality as a whole. It feels terrible to hurt someone or to make a big error at work or school. Here's the thing, though, and we're starting to sound like a broken record, you are responsible not only for your mistake but what you do afterward. Accountability and sincere apology are your first steps to forgiveness and self-forgiveness. Remember when you were a kid and you were sent to your room to think about what you'd done? You need to send yourself to your proverbial room and work things out in your head. What chain of actions led you to commit the error? Why were you so compelled to do so? What changes do you need to make to prevent it from happening again and rebuild trust?

Until you can answer these questions, you will likely not be able to give yourself forgiveness or receive forgiveness from others. But when you can commit an egregious error, take responsibility for your actions, determine the source of your actions and take steps to correct them to prevent further incidents, then you're well on your way to rebuilding your life and your trust with the person you've wronged. The ability to do these things is a great benchmark on your journey to resilience. And if you don't receive forgiveness from others, then you need to go back and think about what we discussed about acceptance. You can't control the actions and reactions of others, only yourself.

Living With Purpose and Hope

That last segment was a bit of a downer, so let's head down the home stretch with some thoughts about positivity and hope. We talked a lot about mindfulness throughout the book, and it's such a buzzword, it can be hard to pinpoint exactly what it means to live a mindful life. Yes, you want to be able to be in touch with your own physical and emotional well-being. But a big part of mindfulness is being in tune with the world around you, and that's seemingly more important than ever these days.

Social dynamics are difficult to master in the 21st century. We hear about cultural appropriation v. cultural appreciation, we deal with issues of race and ethnicity, and we find ourselves living in a time of deeply divided politics. It can be truly difficult to know what to do, what to say, how to act and react, and how to avoid causing unintentional harm to others. The answer is to live with purpose and intent. Mindfulness plays a key role in leading a purposeful life.

Have you ever walked into a room and immediately sensed what the mood of the occupants was? Humans are innately able to feel the emotions of others, but you have to be tuned in. Being purposeful in your mindfulness will heighten your ability to read others. We live in a society where it is increasingly important to be aware of what's going on around us, and the digitalization and globalization of communications brings both a boon of cultural exchange and a burden of being sensitive to the issues surrounding communities other than our own.

Digital communications can also make it difficult to assess a 'mood.' There is, as they say, no font for sarcasm. Tone and intent can be lost through text messages and emails, so it's important to know your audience and remain mindful of your environment, be it virtual or electronic. Think before you type, know who you are speaking with, and when in doubt, it's always best to be more professional than you need to be. Put yourself in the shoes of the person receiving your message, and consider how it would sound to you. When meeting in-person, think before you speak and choose your words carefully and diplomatically.

Mental toughness is not only resilience but mental acuity. Being aware of the feelings of others, being able to assess a social situation, or the mood of the room at work will take you a long way towards living a life that needs no apology. When you care about not only your own feelings but also the feelings of others, you will gain respect. When you gain respect, you gain pride, and when you gain pride, you have higher self-esteem. People with high self-esteem command respect, and thus the cycle continues.

Being mindful and aware of the world around you is also a great way to avoid making the types of external errors that are considered problematic. This mindfulness tells you when you should and when you shouldn't speak. It makes you pause to think about your words before you use them and your actions before you complete them. Mindfulness, that all-important trait of resilient people, is what can stop you from making a mistake before it happens, and if being able to resist the urge to do or say something inappropriate isn't being mentally tough, then we don't know what is!

How Tough Is Tough Enough?

Here we are, nearly to the last segment! You've come so far just by getting here, and we hope you've learned a lot. The last thing to discuss is how to assess your progress with your resiliency goals. We know that mental toughness is something that's difficult to measure, and while the true test comes under stress, there are ways to gauge how you're doing.

A great way to keep a handle on things is to keep a journal or diary. It doesn't need to be an elaborate affair, just something to jot down your thoughts or feelings once or twice a day or notate things that feel important to your goals. If you're tech-minded, there are diary applications for most smartphones, including some specifically designed for tracking emotions and mental health. Some people feel more connected when they write things by hand, but choose whatever method works for you. A journal is also a good place to keep all the notes you make about goal-setting, mission statements and mantras, and self-discovery.

Journaling is a terrific method for tracking how stress affects you over time, and if you are working on building resiliency, you'll have a visual and written record of your progress. When you experience stress or trauma, make a note of it, including what happened, why you felt upset, and how you reacted. As you work on your mindfulness skills and learn to set mental and emotional boundaries, you'll see a change in your reactions and your residual stress. You'll be emotionally equipped to handle almost everything that comes your way.

We say *almost* everything because it is tough to be tough all the time! No matter how hard you work at being mindful, setting boundaries, and taking responsibility for yourself and your behaviors, there is always the human element. You won't always be as strong as you want to be, and it's okay to not be okay. That's when you can rely on your support system and use their positive energy to help you figure things out. The toughest people can be emotionally floored sometimes- losing a parent or other loved one, receiving a bad health diagnosis, or other traumatic events can cause even the most resilient people to stumble.

When you find yourself in a situation like this, allow yourself time to process your emotions. Don't assume that you 'should feel better' after a certain time frame or think that you are failing at being resilient. You aren't! This is where all you've learned about positive self-talk and healthy outlets comes into play. Give yourself what you need to begin healing, and take one day at a time.

Long-term strength and resilience take hard mental and emotional work. Many times, people who are stuck in a negative rut with no immediate way out don't realize just how tough they've been until it's over. If you've ever been in a bad relationship and need to get out or in a job that is taking a toll on your mental health, you know how hard it can be to escape. Things aren't always black and white or cut and dried. Living in a long-term state of high emotional alert affects mental and physical health and creates an unhealthy cycle. When people are in these types of situations, or worse, they often look back and say, "I just did what I had to do." Thus it is with everyday mental toughness. If you say to yourself every morning that you're not only going to get through the day but that you're going to conquer it, you will have great overall success.

So when we say, "How tough is tough enough?" what we really mean is how tough do you need to be to be happy with yourself? In the end, that's all that matters. As long as you are satisfied with your resilience, you haven't compromised your values or your ability to feel sympathy or apathy; then, you're doing just fine. It's always important to make sure that in your pursuit of resilience and toughness, you don't become so tough that you are a detriment to those around you. That's too tough.

Putting It All Together

It's not always about the process; it's about the result. You are going to have good days and bad days because that's just life. No one leads an existence of utter bliss from their birth until the day they die. Even the most privileged fight personal demons, and even the most impoverished can find joy. You are the only one who can decide your own emotional fate. That's what this entire book has been about, and as we wind down, let's recap and reflect on all the key points.

First, you need to be self-aware, be proactive in your positive self-talk, and work on your self-esteem. This is such a crucial part of building resiliency. If you don't know who you are, what you believe in, or how to talk to yourself, how can you relate to others? The exercises in Chapter 2 were designed to help you define yourself. Use them, and use them as often as necessary. Life happens quickly, and what was a priority to you once may not remain a priority. Relationships, jobs, and social circles change, you are allowed to change and evolve with them, as long as you are firm in your principles and don't compromise your values.

Hand in hand with building self-esteem is the need and ability to set boundaries. Boundaries are by nature, protective. They lay out what belongs to you and what belongs to others. In the physical world, they can be walls, fences, or lines drawn on a map. In the professional world, they are set by policies and codes of conduct. In your emotional world, a boundary is whatever you want or need it to be. It signifies to other people that 'this is my part of my heart (brain, life, etc.) that I choose not to share with you.' You have to enforce that boundary; it is not up to other people to enforce it, as much as you want them to respect it.

The respect has to come from within you. In order to set and enforce an emotional boundary, you have to have self-respect. You have to know that you are not deserving of being treated poorly or taken advantage of. You have to respect yourself enough to say that you aren't putting up with anything less than respect from others, and if people cannot help but cross your boundaries, then you have every right to cut them off completely. Trust and respect are not just given; they must be earned. Don't give them out to people who don't deserve them, and don't rent emotional space to anyone who wouldn't do the same for you.

That leads us to the recap of our next point, which is that healthy relationships and support systems are crucial to your own resilience and self-esteem. If you want to find people who love and respect you for who you are, you must first love and respect yourself and rid your life of people who do not, at least to the best of *your* ability. There may always be that one classmate or work colleague with whom you just don't see eye to eye. Be civil and always take the high road.

People are drawn to others who are confident and respectful. When you begin to build healthy relationships and social circles, good will beget good. It's all about finding a way to break out of your negative cycles and into a positive one. It will pay off. The further you distance yourself from the people you've cut back or cut off, the easier it will be to see why they were no good for you. Hindsight is always 20/20, and you'll see manipulators, liars, and users for what they really are.

Live with mindfulness and purpose. We've said it a lot throughout the book, but it is a point that bears repeating. Even in the midst of the worst day, you can find a touchstone with mindfulness. With a simple grounding exercise or recitation of a mantra, you can bring yourself out of your negative emotional state, even if it's just long enough to reset your brain and think about things for a few minutes. It's okay to feel overwhelmed when something traumatic happens. It's your long-term response that matters most.

When you live with a purpose, you are setting yourself up for success, even if there are obstacles or setbacks along the way. Two steps forward and one step back is still one step forward (which makes a good mantra when times are tough, by the way.) You can set goals using the same method you did to set your resiliency goals, by making them specific and attainable. Break big goals down into little pieces. Things always seem more manageable when the steps are smaller. Every task, whether mental, emotional, or physical, can be broken down into chunks. Think about when a small child learns to write a how-to book. They could list every step of making a sandwich or brushing their teeth. There are so many little things that make up every larger task if you only take the time to examine them.

We can't stress enough, though, the importance of mindfulness. Being mindful in all aspects of your life will alleviate so much stress and keep you away from unnecessary awkwardness or ambiguity. Living a mindful life doesn't mean you constantly have to be on high emotional alert, but it does mean that with time, you will pick up on cues from yourself and others that you might not have seen before. Be deliberate in your decision making. Be observant in social and work settings. Choose your words and your actions carefully. If you do all of these things, you will find that you rarely do anything that requires an apology.

Mindfulness also means having control over your behaviors and your emotional reactions. When you live a mindful life, it gives you the upper hand on your feelings. Of course, not many people can escape the occasional visceral response- an exclamation, a nasty look or expression, or something said in anger- these things happen. But being mindful and in touch with your emotions helps you identify what you're feeling and take steps to mitigate negativity. It ties into your self-awareness. Practicing mindfulness leads to being able to determine if you are feeling hurt or angry, sad, jealous, or any other negative emotion, many of which mimic each other and can be confusing. The quicker you can identify your emotions, the quicker you can take steps to address them.

That leads us to our next point to recap, and that's the ability to recognize impermanence. This is the capability to realize that no matter how bad things may seem, they aren't going to be bad forever. Resilient people know that there is always a light at the end of the tunnel, to use an old cliché. This is one of the hardest resiliency skills to learn. It requires rewiring your brain from thinking negatively to thinking positively, despite being faced with overwhelming stress.

There will come a time on your resiliency journey that this sense of impermanence will just seem to pop up out of nowhere. One day, you'll think to yourself, "Okay, this stinks, but it won't always be like this!" It will probably surprise you when it happens. The truth is, it isn't something that happens overnight, but it is something that doesn't arise until it's needed. Once you discover that you've gained this ability, use it. Use it every day that you need to get through what you need to get through. The knowledge that things WILL get better can be a lifeline in tough times and even everyday stress.

If you are in a situation that you need to get out of, cling to that lifeline and use your other skills to make the decisions you need to make to improve things for yourself. If you're having a mental health crisis, tell yourself that you won't always feel like this, and then take steps to seek help. Lean on your support system to get you the assistance you need. The same goes for being a bad domestic situation. Use the resources available to you, like the crisis hotline or local agencies, to find a way to get out safely. If you're stuck in a job that is draining the life out of you, figure out what you need to do to find better employment. Set goals, break down tasks, and get yourself sorted.

Few things in this life are permanent, even grief and anger. Once the shock wears off, you can work through these emotions and find your way to the other side. If you need help, ask for it. There is greater strength and resilience in asking for help than trying to go it alone. Please don't let stigma stop you from getting the assistance you need. You are worth it! Find strength in the journey and in the people around you. Even if it's your own actions that led you down a path of negativity, you deserve to bring yourself back out of the darkness.

On that note, we can recap our discussions about mistakes and how to be resilient enough to move past them. It takes a strong person to be accountable for their actions, apologize, and try to make amends. After all, isn't that one of the major themes of this whole book? Personal responsibility is a cornerstone of being resilient. When you've got no one to blame yourself, you have to put the work into bouncing back. This goes for anything you may have done to hurt yourself, your loved ones, your colleagues, or your friends. Ask for forgiveness, and be grateful when you receive it. Outline what steps you'll be taking to rectify the problem. Show others that you know you messed up, you have reconciled this with yourself, and you are actively going to be doing what needs to be done to assure it doesn't happen again. If you can do this, you will greatly improve your chances of receiving forgiveness and regaining trust. Even if you do not, you will at least receive some respect.

Be judicious in the way you forgive others as well. Set the appropriate boundaries and stick to them until you feel they can be adjusted. As the old saying goes, "Fool me once, shame on you. Fool me twice, shame on me!" If you are working on rebuilding trust with someone, from either side, be respectful and firm on boundaries until it is proven that they can be expanded or crossed. Don't compromise your feelings or values at the insistence of someone else (Hear that kids? Say no to peer pressure!) because they are feeling 'hurt by your boundaries.' If they hadn't violated your trust, the boundary wouldn't be necessary. Remember your self-worth.

Remember that there isn't always a right answer or an answer at all! Being able to accept that some things cannot be changed is one of our last topics, but no less important. Way back in Chapter 1, we talked about admitting ignorance, and earlier in this chapter, we went over the acceptance of things we cannot change. These concepts are related, and if you can do both, you are well on your way to mental toughness. If you admit that you don't know something, you can then take steps to remedy that. Learn and grow from your ignorance or lack of skill. If you examine the situation, and there is nothing to learn or nothing to do, you need to accept that and move on.

Moving on and moving forward are so crucial to being resilient. The ability to say that you've done everything you can and it's time to let go is a really good feeling. So, too, is knowing that no matter what happens, you are strong enough to make it through the storm. Be kind to yourself. Don't forget to use your healthy outlets and lean on your support system. Give and receive forgiveness when needed, and set boundaries that show your respect for your own worth. Define, revisit, achieve, and adjust your goals as needed, and take time to recognize your values and beliefs. Be mindful, thoughtful, and deliberate in your thoughts, actions, and words, and most of all, give yourself time to grow.

We've come so far together through these chapters, and now it's time to put all your new knowledge to good use! Get a journal and get ready for some serious self-evaluation. You're going to learn so much about yourself just in the process of working through those exercises! Practice your mindfulness exercises, and live with a hopeful heart, every day. Don't forget to take care of yourself and be accountable for your actions, and your actions alone. You are the only person you can control. Be proud of what you do with that power. Best of luck on your resiliency journey. We believe in you, now go ahead and start believing in yourself!

CONCLUSION

Thanks for reading *Mental Toughness for Beginners*. We hope you learned everything you need to know to get started on your way to resiliency for everyday living and for the long-term. The lessons in this book can be applied to so many other areas of your life, too. You can use the goal-setting skills for anything you set your mind to, and writing mission statements and mantras can help you stick to any plan.

Being mindful is also something that can carry you through so many areas of your life. The ability to read a social or professional setting before speaking or acting is a great exercise in both mindfulness and self-discipline. Mindfulness connects you to yourself and the world around you in ways that will pay dividends and earn you respect from your inner circle and beyond.

The ability to take personal responsibility, recognize mistakes, and take steps to correct them is also something that is going to help you gain both respect from others and respect from yourself. Accountability is crucial to being tough. It takes so much strength to say, "I'm sorry" and mean it. It takes even more strength to find a way to learn and grow from your mistakes. It takes EVEN more strength to make amends, rebuild trust, and move forward. You can be proud of yourself for attempting these things, and even prouder when you achieve them.

Another key takeaway from the book is acceptance- of yourself, of others, and of immovable situations. When you can develop the skills needed to be accepting, you are going to find a happier, more resilient resistance. You will have so much more positive energy that you can spend working on things that you can change, and you will do great things! When we stop focusing on the things we cannot control and put our efforts into the things that we can, we move forward. Life itself is about moving forward, and when you do so with acceptance and positivity, the mental strength you are seeking will follow suit.

Mental Toughness for Beginners was written as a guidebook for you to get from where you are to where you want to be. The lessons outlined are here for you to use, not once, but again and again when you need a refresher or some assurance that you're doing okay. We hope you'll revisit the chapters often to give yourself a boost of positivity and remind yourself that life is a journey. Take the words and guidance in this book and use them to become the best, strongest you that you can be. It's not a sprint, it's a marathon, and you can take as long as you need to learn.

We hope that you'll use *Mental Toughness for Beginners* now and for a long time to come. The topics we've discussed are timeless despite the onward march of technology. So, be self-aware and accountable. Lean on your friends and family, and give those energy vampires the boot! Take responsibility for your actions, make amends with those you've hurt, and if it's merited, forgive those who've hurt you. You'll feel better when you're not carrying negativity in your heart and mind. Shrink your mountains into molehills, and shrink your heavy tasks into little steps. Write your mission statements and your mantras, practice your mindfulness, and most of all- love yourself! The best thing you can do to build resilience is to know and like who you are, because then, no one can get you down. Don't forget to use your healthy stress outlets and have a little fun along the way!

Thanks once again for reading *Mental Toughness for Beginners*. Dig deep, know thyself, and enjoy your path to a resilient life!

DESCRIPTION

Have you ever thought to yourself, "I need to toughen up"? Have you been dealing with stress and trauma in an unhealthy way, and you're just not sure how to break the cycle? Do you just sometimes feel like others would like and respect you better if you could like and respect yourself a bit more? If you're stuck in a negative rut, can't see your way out, and want to learn how to live a happier, more purposeful life while kicking stress to the curb, then *Mental Toughness for Beginners* is the book for you!

In this book, readers will learn:

- the common traits of mentally tough people
- how identifying your values and beliefs can define your personality
- how to boost your self-esteem with positive self-talk
- what it means to be mindful and how to use mindfulness exercises
- how mindfulness can improve your life and the lives of others around you
- what role personal accountability plays in being resilient
- the difference between stifling negative emotions and using healthy outlets
- how to accept things that cannot be changed
- how to build a support system and rely on that system in times of need
- how grief works and why it is a necessary tool for good mental health
- what emotional boundaries are, how to set them, and when to adjust them
- why accountability is so important to building resilience
- why it's okay to not always be okay, and how to improve your outlook
- how to set and stick to goals with mission statements and mantras
- why a journal is a useful tool for tracking emotional responses and stress reactions
- and much more!

Mental Toughness for Beginners addresses the big internal questions, asking the reader to do a deep, internal dive to think about their strengths and weaknesses, discern their beliefs and values, and examine what it is about themselves that's holding them back from achieving resiliency. The book also addresses tough issues like loss and family dysfunction, how to find the strength to rise above these issues, and what to do when nothing can be done.

The book gives detailed exercises for mindfulness and meditation and gives real-life examples and analogies that are relatable and down-to-earth. *Mental Toughness for Beginners* also gives the reader insight into setting emotional boundaries, forgiveness, and acceptance, and talks about the difference between moving forward and moving on. Each chapter is broken down into easy-to-digest segments that can be read and reread as a primer and a guidebook.

If you're ready to get started or take your self-awareness, self-esteem, and resiliency to the next level, then *Mental Toughness for Beginners* needs to be your next read. Get your copy today and discover the strength within you. You can learn to handle stress and anxiety, live a mindful and purposeful life, and discover the secret to breaking the cycle of negativity in your life, for good! Why wait? Change your life today!